THE ATHENIAN

EBURY
PRESS

TIM VASILAKIS

Hello! Welcome to *The Athenian Cookbook*! I'm excited to share with you the recipes I grew up with. It's an honour to be part of your kitchen, so thank you! I hope that this book serves as the foundation to learning how to cook tasty and healthy Greek recipes. You will learn how to cook the most well-known dishes of the Greek cuisine, from Athens to our beautiful islands. My hope and aim is that this cookbook will place Greek cuisine on the global food map, alongside other well-established cuisines.

A little bit about me; I was born and raised in Athens, where I grew up in a typically urban Athenian neighbourhood. Loads of concrete, very urban, very much home. From a young age I was surrounded by all types of Greek cuisine, and I'd very happily eat whatever I was offered (even things that kids wouldn't usually choose, like Greek lentil soup and all types of fish). I spent summers on Chios, the island in the Aegean where my dad is from. The food was amazing: seafood, salads, vegetables, everything fresh. I remember going fishing with my mum, being on this tiny boat out in the open sea, catching some fish and sailing home, cleaning and cooking it, with fresh veg from my auntie's farm. Looking back, it was an incredible thing to have experienced.

Fast-forward to me leaving Athens at 18, when I went to study in Edinburgh, then London. It was there that I fell in love with street food, which back in the early 2010s was just starting to be a thing. I loved that you could travel to every continent in the world in a lunch hour and eat all this incredible food. But there was no Greek food at all – finding authentic Greek food in London was really tough. So I started experimenting at home, just to satisfy my own cravings. First were the dishes my mum used to cook at home when I was growing up, then I moved on to perfecting gyros and souvlaki (my absolute favourite).

Spending all that time in street-food markets really planted a seed and I thought, 'Why don't I start a stall?' I'd always wanted to run my own business, and this was my 'now or never' moment. So back in 2014 I ran my first stall at a tiny market in North London, then a month later I moved to Brick Lane, one of the city's busiest markets. The rest, as they say, is history.

The Athenian has always been about making Greek food accessible to as many people as possible. The idea is for everyone to see modern Athens and Greek cuisine as I see it, to discover Greek food as it really is, and to come on a journey to this amazing city. It's one that's not about stereotypical Greece at all, but all about modern Athens, and living and eating the Athenian way. With this cookbook, I hope to bring that into people's kitchens and homes, with simple recipes that are a joy to make – and even better to eat.

Kali Orexi!
Καλή Όρεξη!

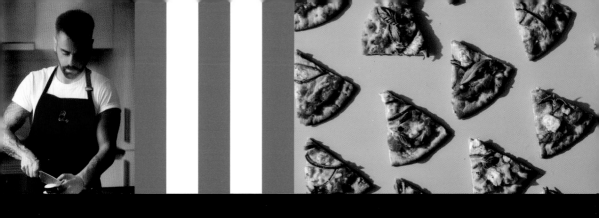

I WANT TO BRING MODERN ATHENS INTO PEOPLE'S HOMES, WITH SIMPLE RECIPES THAT ARE A JOY TO MAKE – AND EVEN BETTER TO EAT.

LIKE ATHENS.
BUT HERE.

Our little owl has flown a long way since 2014, growing from a humble market stall to a fast-expanding network of restaurants and locations, in next to no time. Now, people all over the world get to savour Athens today – and experience Greek food made the Athenian way. That little owl has picked up some awards on the journey, but really, it wouldn't have got very far at all without our incredible customers and the amazing team of Athenians, led by founder Tim Vasilakis.

From that very first day on the market stall it's always been about the food. Nothing but the best ingredients for dishes freshly and lovingly made to order right there in front of you, for a big hit of taste and flavour. Souvlaki and gyros made to our secret recipe, small-batch halloumi, handmade dips, antioxidant-rich oregano, plant-based options. We source everything from our long-time partners in Greece and those local to our restaurants, so we know where every single ingredient comes from. No cut corners, no compromises.

When it comes to doing what's right for the world around us, we step up. There's no plastic in our packaging, our cooking oil is turned into biodiesel, and our kitchens run on renewable energy. We like to do our bit for charity, too, so we partner with a different one every three months. It means eating Athenian makes a difference to charities doing great things for people all over the world.

For us, it's the Athenian way. And it's all part of our vision: making Greek food accessible and bringing people on a journey to see modern Athens through our eyes. It's the Athens we know and love: unpretentious and unapologetic. Athenians of today are all about the moment – the here and now. So we're proud to bring you the hottest food from the coolest city, right into your kitchen, right here and now.

CONTENTS

FUNDA-MENTALS

ΤΑ ΒΑΣΙΚΑ

YOGHURT SAUCE

**MAKES APPROX.
200ML /7FL OZ
(SCANT 1 CUP) SAUCE
PREP: 10 MINUTES**

1 garlic clove
½ tsp sea salt
grated zest of 1 lemon
1 tbsp lemon juice
1 tbsp olive oil
200g/7oz (scant 1 cup)
   Greek yoghurt
a few sprigs of mint,
   finely chopped
freshly ground black
   pepper

You can serve this versatile yoghurt sauce with grilled (broiled) kebabs, chicken, fish, roasted vegetables or meatballs. Or serve it as a dip for oregano or halloumi fries (see pages 98 and 20), or vegetable fritters (see pages 16 and 18).

1 Crush the garlic with the sea salt using a pestle and mortar.

2 Transfer to a bowl and stir in the lemon zest and juice and olive oil.

3 Add the yoghurt and mint and stir until smooth and well combined. Grind in some black pepper and check the seasoning, adding more salt or garlic to taste, if wished. If the sauce is too thick for your liking, thin it with a little water.

4 Store in an airtight container in the fridge. It will keep well for 2–3 days.

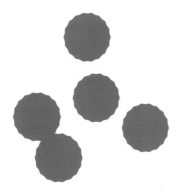

VARIATIONS
• Use dried mint instead of fresh.
• Dust with paprika (sweet or smoked).
• Stir in a little tahini.

GREEK SALAD DRESSING

LADOLEMONO

120ml/4fl oz (½ cup) extra
   virgin Greek olive oil
juice of 1 large lemon
a pinch of dried oregano
   or mint
sea salt and freshly ground
   black pepper

The classic dressing for green salads and *horiatiki* (Greek village salad) is a simple blend of fruity green olive oil and lemon juice flavoured with dried herbs. You can also use this to dress a warm potato salad (see page 109), cooked beans, broccoli and greens as well as fish and seafood (see note below).

1 Whisk together the olive oil and lemon juice in a bowl.

2 Stir in the dried herbs and season to taste with salt and pepper.

VARIATIONS
- Add a crushed garlic clove or some grated lemon zest.
- Add chopped fresh mint, oregano, dill or Greek basil.
- Sweeten with a dash of Greek thyme honey.
- Stir in some honey mustard for a thicker, creamier salad dressing.

SEAFOOD DRESSING

Omit the dried herbs and use this for dressing grilled (broiled) white fish, prawns (shrimp), lobster and seafood.

SOUVLAKI SAUCE

MAKES APPROX.
150ML/5FL OZ
(GENEROUS ½ CUP)
PREP: 10 MINUTES

115g/4oz (½ cup) thick
   Greek yoghurt
3 tbsp mayonnaise
3 tbsp Dijon mustard
1 heaped tbsp clear
   Greek honey
1 garlic clove, crushed
sea salt and freshly ground
   black pepper
smoked or sweet paprika,
   for dusting

Serve this creamy aromatic sauce with grilled (broiled) souvlaki or gyros (see pages 32–45). Use a really yellow mustard for a lovely deep colour.

1 Mix the yoghurt, mayonnaise and mustard together in a small bowl until thick and creamy.

2 Stir in the honey and crushed garlic. Check the seasoning, adding black pepper and some salt, if needed.

3 Dust with paprika, then cover with some kitchen foil (aluminum foil) or clingfilm (plastic wrap) and chill in the fridge until required. This will keep well for 4–5 days.

VARIATIONS
- Use a yellow English mustard instead of Dijon.
- If you have a sweet tooth, add some more honey to taste.
- Stir in a dash of lemon juice.

HANDMADE GREEK PITA BREADS

MAKES 4
PREP: 20 MINUTES
RISE: 1½ HOURS
COOK: 8–10 MINUTES

300g/10oz (3 cups) plain (all-purpose) flour, plus extra for dusting
2 tsp salt
2 tsp sugar
4 tsp active dry yeast
480ml/16fl oz (2 cups) warm water
2 tbsp olive oil, plus extra for shallow-frying
dried oregano, for sprinkling

Image on page 6

Nothing beats a real homemade pita – the commercially made ones you buy in supermarkets just can't compete. The hands-on time is only 20 minutes, so you can get on with your chores or just relax while the dough is rising.

1 Put the flour, salt, sugar and yeast in a bowl and mix together. Make a well in the centre and add half of the warm water. Mix well and then slowly add the remaining water, stirring until everything combines into a ball of dough. Pour the olive oil over the ball and turn until it's covered all over with oil.

2 Cover the bowl with clingfilm (plastic wrap) or a clean cloth and leave to rest at room temperature for 1½ hours, or until the dough rises and doubles in size.

3 Preheat the oven to 170°C/325°F/gas mark 3.

4 Cut the dough into 4 equal-sized pieces. Place one on a lightly floured surface and roll out lightly into a circle, approximately 18cm/7in diameter, or just stretch and shape it with your hands. If the dough is too sticky, dust with a little flour – it should feel soft and fluffy. Repeat with the other pieces of dough to make 4 pitas.

5 Place the pitas on 2 baking trays and cook in the preheated oven for 5–7 minutes until they firm up and are slightly darker in colour. Do not let them brown at this stage.

6 Lightly oil a large frying pan (skillet) and set over a medium heat. When it's hot, fry the pitas, in batches, for 1 minute on each side until golden.

7 Remove from the pan and sprinkle with oregano. Serve warm with souvlaki, gyros and kebabs or cut into quarters to serve with dips.

Tip: If you stretch and shape the pitas with your hands instead of rolling them out, they will be lighter and fluffier.

MEZE & SNACKS

ΜΕΖΕΔΑΚΙΑ

STUFFED VINE LEAVES

DOLMADES

25 vine leaves in brine,
  drained and rinsed
olive oil, for brushing and
  drizzling
juice of 2 lemons, plus extra
  for serving
Greek yoghurt, to serve
  (optional)

STUFFING:
2 tbsp olive oil
2 onions, finely chopped
1 garlic clove, crushed
225g/8oz (1 cup) risotto
  rice, e.g. arborio
600ml/1 pint (2½ cups)
  water
2 tomatoes, diced
a small handful of dill,
  chopped
½ tsp dried oregano
50g/2oz (generous ¼ cup)
  currants
50g/2oz (½ cup) pine nuts
sea salt and freshly ground
  black pepper

Dolmades are served in a variety of sizes from medium-sized ones eaten as an appetizer, to smaller ones served as a *meze* dish or snack, to tiny ones no larger than the end of a little (pinky) finger. They can be filled with minced (ground) beef or rice flavoured with herbs. If you are lucky enough to have fresh vine leaves, blanch them in boiling water for 2 minutes before filling them.

1 To make the stuffing, heat the oil in a large frying pan (skillet) set over a medium–high heat. Cook the onions and garlic, stirring occasionally, for 5 minutes, until just tender.

2 Stir in the rice and cook for 1 minute, then add the water and bring to the boil. Reduce the heat and cook for 5–10 minutes, or until the rice is half-cooked and most of the liquid has been absorbed. Stir in the tomatoes, herbs, currants, pine nuts and seasoning. Leave to cool.

3 Take a vine leaf and place it, vein-side up, on a clean work surface. Flatten it and put a dessertspoon of stuffing in the centre. Fold the sides over the top and roll up tightly to make a sausage shape. Repeat with the remaining vine leaves and stuffing.

4 Brush a little olive oil over the bottom of a large, deep, heavy-based saucepan and cover with any torn or leftover vine leaves. Place a layer of *dolmades*, seam-side down, on top, packing them in tightly. Keep layering them up in this way. Pour over the lemon juice and enough hot water to just cover them. Place a small plate on top to stop them moving.

5 Simmer over a low–medium heat for 45 minutes, or until the rice is cooked and tender. Turn off the heat and leave the *dolmades* in the pan until they are lukewarm or cold and then remove them with a slotted spoon.

6 Serve the *dolmades* drizzled with olive oil and lemon juice with some yoghurt on the side, if you like. They will keep well for several days, stored in an airtight container, in the fridge.

Tip: The uncooked dolmades can be frozen for up to 2 months.

VARIATIONS
- Add a pinch of ground cinnamon to the stuffing.
- Serve them in a pool of *avgolemono* sauce (see page 88).

COURGETTE FRITTERS

KOLOKYTHOKEFTEDES

SERVES 2–3
PREP: 20 MINUTES
DRAIN: 30 MINUTES
COOK: 4 MINUTES

1 large courgette (zucchini), coarsely grated
¼ tbsp sea salt
1 bunch flat-leaf (Italian) parsley, chopped
1 bunch of mint, chopped
1 red onion, chopped
60g/2oz (½ cup) diced feta cheese
1 medium free-range egg
¼ tsp freshly ground black pepper
30g/1oz (½ cup) fresh white breadcrumbs
120ml/4fl oz (½ cup) olive oil, for frying
Greek yoghurt or tzatziki (see page 24), to serve

Golden and crispy on the outside and deliciously soft and moist when you bite into them, these fritters are one of our Athenian favourites. They are easy to make at home and perfect for freezing (see tip below).

1 Place the grated courgette in a bowl and sprinkle with the salt. Mix well, then set aside for the liquid to drain away for 30 minutes. Squeeze out any excess liquid with your hands and pat dry the courgette with kitchen paper (paper towels).

2 Put the courgette in a clean, dry bowl with the herbs, red onion, feta, egg, black pepper and breadcrumbs. Mix well until everything comes together. If the mixture is too damp, add some more breadcrumbs to bind up.

3 Divide the mixture into 6 or 8 equal-sized portions and mould each one into a ball.

4 Heat the olive oil in a large frying pan (skillet) set over a medium heat and fry the keftedes for 2 minutes on each side until crisp and golden brown. Remove with a slotted spoon and drain on kitchen paper (paper towels).

5 Serve piping hot with Greek yoghurt or tzatziki on the side.

Tip: You can make double the quantity and place the uncooked balls on a lightly floured tray in the freezer for 1 day before transferring to a sealed plastic bag and freezing for up to 1 month. Defrost for 20 minutes before frying as above.

VARIATION
To make courgette (zucchini) burgers, form the mixture into 2 or 3 patties and brush lightly with beaten egg before dipping them into breadcrumbs. Bake in a preheated oven at 180°C/350°F/gas mark 4 for 45 minutes.

TOMATO FRITTERS

DOMATOKEFTEDES

5 medium ripe vine
   tomatoes
1 red onion, chopped
1 bunch of mint, chopped
6 basil leaves, chopped
1 tsp dried oregano
85g/3oz (1½ cups) fresh
   white breadcrumbs
1 tsp salt
¼ tsp freshly ground black
   pepper
120ml/4fl oz (½ cup) olive
   oil, for frying
chopped parsley, for
   sprinkling
200g/7oz (scant 1 cup)
   Greek yoghurt
¼ tsp smoked paprika
sprigs of mint, to garnish

Delicious plant-based tomato fritters are a speciality of the Aegean island of Santorini and they have become an Athenian classic dish for us, too. For the best flavour, use the sweetest tomatoes you can find.

1 With a sharp knife, make a cross in the bottom of each tomato and lower them into a pan of boiling water. Reduce the heat and simmer for 5 minutes or until the skins split and start to peel. Remove the tomatoes with a slotted spoon and plunge into a bowl of ice-cold water to cool them down quickly.

2 Skin the tomatoes, scoop out and discard the seeds and any excess liquid, then dice the flesh.

3 Put the tomato flesh in a bowl with the onion, herbs, breadcrumbs, salt and pepper. Mix well until everything comes together. If the mixture is too damp and crumbly, add some more breadcrumbs to bind it.

4 Divide the mixture into 6 or 8 equal-sized portions and mould each one into a ball.

5 Heat the olive oil in a large frying pan (skillet) set over a medium heat and fry the keftedes for 2 minutes on each side until crisp and golden. Remove with a slotted spoon and drain on kitchen paper (paper towels).

6 Serve hot, sprinkled with parsley, with some Greek yoghurt dusted with smoked paprika and garnished with mint sprigs.

VARIATIONS
- Serve with pre-dinner drinks, as part of a *meze* platter or as a tasty snack.
- Add some chopped fresh dill.

Tip: To cool the tomatoes fast, add some ice cubes to the bowl of water.

SPICY FETA DIP

TIROKAFTERI

300g/10oz feta cheese, diced
2 red (bell) peppers, deseeded and roasted
1 tbsp olive oil
½ tsp dried red chilli flakes
100g/3½oz (scant ½ cup) Greek yoghurt
thinly sliced red chilli and thyme or oregano leaves, to garnish (optional)

This spicy, salty dip is the perfect accompaniment to oregano halloumi fries (see page 20), warm pita bread triangles, raw vegetable dippers or sesame breadsticks and savoury crackers.

1 Blitz the feta, red peppers, olive oil and chilli flakes until smooth in a sturdy blender or food processor.

2 Transfer to a bowl and add the yoghurt. Mix well until smooth and creamy.

3 Sprinkle with red chilli and herbs (if using) and serve with pita bread.

See image on page 21

Tip: Instead of roasting the peppers yourself, use bottled roasted or grilled red peppers in olive oil and drain well before adding to the other ingredients.

VARIATIONS
• Add a small garlic clove.
• Use it as an alternative to mayonnaise in sandwiches.

OREGANO HALLOUMI FRIES

150g/5oz (1 cup) rice flour
½ tsp sea salt
1 tsp ground cumin
1 tsp dried oregano
½ tsp grated lemon zest
350g/12oz halloumi
120ml/4fl oz (½ cup) olive oil, for frying
spicy feta dip (see page 19), to serve
chopped flat-leaf (Italian) parsley, for sprinkling

These halloumi fries are the simplest, tastiest and quickest you'll ever make. And you don't have to be a vegetarian to enjoy them. Serve them as a snack, a 'side' or rolled into a pita with some shredded lettuce, sliced tomato and red onion, drizzled with souvlaki sauce.

1 Put the flour, salt, cumin, oregano and lemon zest in a bowl and mix well together.

2 Slice the cheese lengthways into fingers (like chips) and dip each one quickly into a small bowl of cold water, then into the flour mixture.

3 Heat the oil in a large frying pan (skillet) set over a medium heat. Add the battered halloumi and fry for 2 minutes on each side until crisp and golden brown. Remove and drain on kitchen paper (paper towels).

4 Serve the halloumi fries immediately while they're piping hot with the spicy feta dip, sprinkled with parsley.

Tip: Vegans can use vegan, dairy-free halloumi to make these delicious fries.

VARIATIONS
- Substitute firm feta cheese cut into fingers for the halloumi.
- Add some freshly ground black pepper.
- Drizzle the fries with hot sauce, e.g. sriracha.

YELLOW SPLIT PEA DIP

SERVES 4
PREP: 10 MINUTES
COOK: 1 HOUR

FAVA

200g/7oz (scant 1 cup) yellow split peas (dry weight)
½ red onion, chopped
1 tbsp olive oil, plus extra for drizzling
½ tsp sea salt
capers and thinly sliced or diced red onion, to garnish

This earthy dip is packed with protein and healthy vitamins and minerals. Serve it as a snack, *meze* dish or an appetizer with a traditional garnish of capers and red onion, or why not try the delicious caramelized onion topping opposite?

1 Rinse the split peas in a sieve under a running cold tap. Put them in a large pan with twice the amount of cold water to cover them – about 400ml/14fl oz (1¾ cups). Add the red onion, olive oil and salt.

2 Set the pan over a high heat and bring to the boil. Reduce the heat to low–medium and cook gently for 1 hour or until the split peas are softened and tender and most of the water has been absorbed, so you end up with a thick broth. Remove from the heat and leave to cool.

3 Using a hand-held immersion blender, blend the mixture until thick and smooth. Alternatively, blitz in a food processor.

4 Transfer the *fava* to a serving bowl and drizzle with olive oil. Top with the capers and some sliced or diced red onion. Serve as a dip with warm pita bread.

VARIATIONS
- Add a little grated lemon zest to the fava and serve drizzled with lemon juice.
- Add 2 garlic cloves to the pan before cooking the split peas.
- Garnish with fresh oregano or thyme leaves.
- Dust with smoked paprika.

Tip: For a coarser, more grainy texture, use a potato masher instead of a blender.

CARAMELIZED ONION TOPPING

3 tbsp olive oil
2 onions, thinly sliced
a good pinch of sugar
2 tbsp red wine vinegar
sea salt and freshly ground black pepper

1 Heat the oil in a large frying pan (skillet) set over a low–medium heat. Cook the onions, stirring occasionally, for 15 minutes or until meltingly tender and golden brown. Stir in the sugar and vinegar to taste.

2 Continue cooking for 5–10 minutes until sticky and caramelized. Season to taste and use as a topping for the *fava*.

GREEK YOGHURT DIP

SERVES 4
PREP: 15 MINUTES

TZATZIKI

1 medium cucumber
1 garlic clove, grated
350g/12oz (1½ cups)
   Greek yoghurt
½ tsp sea salt
1 tbsp olive oil

Why buy ready-made tzatziki in the supermarket when you can make the real thing so quickly and easily yourself? Cool and refreshing, it's not only a wonderful dip but also great for spooning on to souvlaki, gyros, grilled (broiled) meat and chicken or roasted vegetables. You can even dilute it with water and extra yoghurt to make a sauce or a chilled summer soup, or you can make a colourful pink version using beetroot (see below).

1 Grate the cucumber coarsely and put it in a colander. Use your hands to squeeze out any excess water.

2 Transfer it to a bowl and add the grated garlic and yoghurt. Mix well until the mixture is smooth and creamy.

3 Stir in the salt and olive oil and serve with pita or crusty bread.

VARIATIONS
- If you like garlic, use 2 large cloves.
- Add a dash of red wine vinegar or some grated lemon zest.

VEGAN TZATZIKI

You can easily adapt this recipe to make a vegan tzatziki. Just substitute dairy-free vegan yoghurt (made with soya milk, almond milk, oat milk or coconut milk or cream) for dairy and follow the recipe above.

BEETROOT TZATZIKI

SERVES 3–4 | PREP: 10 MINUTES

400g/14oz boiled
   beetroot (beets), peeled
1 garlic clove, grated
250g/9oz (1 cup) Greek
   yoghurt

1 tbsp olive oil
¼ tsp sea salt
chopped dill, to garnish
   (optional)

1 Put all the ingredients in a food processor or blender and blitz until smooth and creamy.

2 Transfer to a serving bowl, sprinkle with dill (optional) and serve with warm pita triangles.

AUBERGINE DIP

SERVES 4
PREP: 10 MINUTES
COOK: 1 HOUR

MELITZANOSALATA

2 large aubergines
  (eggplants)
1 garlic clove, peeled
1 tbsp fresh white
  breadcrumbs
3 tbsp olive oil, plus extra
  for drizzling
1 tbsp red wine vinegar
a handful of flat-leaf
  (Italian) parsley, chopped
sea salt, to taste

This traditional Greek dip is served with crusty bread or warm pita as a sharing *meze* dish, or it can be eaten with meatballs or simple grilled (broiled) meat.

1 Preheat the oven to 180°C/350°F/gas mark 4. Line a baking tray with baking parchment.

2 Pierce the aubergines several times with a fork and place on the lined baking tray. Bake in the preheated oven for 1 hour, or until soft.

3 When the aubergines are cool enough to handle, peel them over a colander, letting the flesh fall into the colander. Leave for 15 minutes to drain away the bitter liquid.

4 If you want a creamy dip, blitz the aubergine flesh with the garlic, breadcrumbs, olive oil and vinegar in a blender or food processor. If it's too loose, add a few more breadcrumbs. If you want a more textured dip, chop the aubergine and place in a bowl. Blend everything else and then mix with the chopped aubergine.

5 Stir in half of the parsley and season to taste with salt. Serve drizzled with olive oil and sprinkled with the remaining parsley.

Tip: If you're in a hurry you can grill (broil) the aubergines instead of baking them in the oven.

VARIATIONS
- Garnish with chopped spring onions (scallions) and diced tomato or red (bell) pepper.
- Add some lemon juice to taste.
- Add a roasted red pepper and blitz with the other ingredients.

SHRIMP SAGANAKI

GARIDES SAGANAKI

SERVES 4
PREP: 10 MINUTES
COOK: 25–30
MINUTES

2 tbsp olive oil
½ small red onion, finely
    chopped
2 garlic cloves, crushed
4 ripe tomatoes, chopped
60ml/2fl oz (¼ cup) dry
    white wine
a pinch of sugar
a few sprigs of flat-leaf
    (Italian) parsley, chopped
450g/1lb large raw prawns
    (jumbo shrimp), shelled,
    deveined and tails intact
100g/3½oz feta cheese
sea salt and freshly ground
    black pepper

If you've never tried seafood with cheese, this is the recipe that will convert you. It's a taverna classic and perfect for warm summer days. It's usually eaten as a *mezede* along with other sharing dishes. For the best results, use good-quality fresh or frozen and thawed raw prawns (shrimp), not precooked ones, which won't be so juicy and succulent.

1 Preheat the oven to 200°C/400°F/gas mark 6.

2 Heat the olive oil in an ovenproof flameproof dish or frying pan (skillet) set over a medium heat. Cook the onion and garlic, stirring occasionally, for 6–8 minutes, until softened. Add the tomatoes and cook for 5 minutes, stirring occasionally, until they soften and thicken.

3 Add the wine and sugar and cook for 5 minutes until the sauce reduces and thickens. Season to taste with salt and pepper.

4 Reduce the heat to low and add the parsley and prawns. Cook gently for 1–2 minutes on each side or until they turn pink.

5 Crumble the feta over the top and bake in the preheated oven for 10 minutes, or until the cheese starts to melt into the sauce.

6 Serve immediately while it's piping hot with crusty bread or pita bread to mop up the tomato sauce.

VARIATIONS
- For a more intense tomato sauce, add some tomato paste.
- Instead of white wine, add a little ouzo.
- If you want to eat this as a main course, serve with boiled rice.

Tip: If you leave the heads on the prawns, the sauce will be tastier.

CHEESY FILO TRIANGLES

**MAKES 16
PREP: 30 MINUTES
COOK: 15–20
MINUTES**

TIROPITAKIA

200g/7oz feta cheese, crumbled
200g/7oz (1 cup) ricotta cheese
3 small free-range eggs
¼ tsp sea salt (less if the feta is very salty)
freshly ground black pepper
8 sheets filo (phyllo) pastry
olive oil or melted unsalted butter, for brushing

These popular little cheese pies are on sale in bakeries, tavernas and restaurants all over the Greek mainland and islands. They are easy to make and freeze well, so why not make several batches and keep some unbaked ones in the freezer? Bake them from frozen for 20 minutes.

1 Preheat the oven to 180°C/350°F/gas mark 4. Line a baking sheet with parchment paper.

2 In a bowl, mix the feta and ricotta together. Beat the eggs until they are fluffy and stir into the cheese mixture with the salt and a grinding of black pepper, mixing until well combined.

3 Spread out one sheet of filo pastry on a clean work surface and brush lightly with olive oil or melted butter. Place another pastry sheet on top and brush with oil or butter. Cut lengthways into 4 long strips of equal width.

4 Place a spoonful of the filling at the end of one strip and fold the corner of the filo pastry over the top to make a triangle that covers the filling. Fold it over again and continue from side to side until you reach the end of the strip and have a neat triangular parcel. Repeat with the other strips and place the filo triangles on the lined baking sheet.

5 Repeat the process with the remaining filo pastry and filling until everything is used up. You should end up with 16 filo triangles. Brush them with oil or melted butter.

6 Bake in the preheated oven for 15–20 minutes, or until the filo is crispy and golden brown. Remove and set aside to cool before serving.

VARIATIONS
- Use cottage cheese or grated Graviera instead of ricotta.
- Add some chopped mint or dill to the filling.

Tip: Always thaw frozen filo pastry overnight in the fridge, not at room temperature. And don't open the package until you're ready to use it. When you're working with filo pastry it's important to prevent it drying out and cracking. Keep the unused sheets covered with a damp tea towel (dish cloth) while you work.

FRIED CALAMARI

KALAMARAKIA TIGANITA

SERVES 4
PREP: 10 MINUTES
COOK: 6–8 MINUTES

675g/1½lb fresh squid
(or frozen and thawed),
cleaned and washed
85g/3oz (¾ cup) plain
(all-purpose) flour
½ tsp sea salt, plus extra
for sprinkling
freshly ground black
pepper
vegetable oil, for frying
lemon wedges, for
squeezing

For most people, fried squid is the food that triggers fond memories of Greek summers and long lazy lunches in beach tavernas. The good news is that you can cook it yourself at home. It's so quick and easy and there aren't many ingredients.

1 Cut the squid into rings, about 1cm/½in wide, and lightly blot them, together with the tentacles, with kitchen paper (paper towels). They should be slightly damp but not too wet.

2 Mix the flour with the salt and pepper in a bowl. Dip the squid into the seasoned flour until coated all over, then shake off any excess flour and set aside while you heat the oil.

3 Pour the oil into a deep frying pan (skillet) to a depth of 5cm/2in and set over a medium–high heat. When it's very hot, drop a squid ring into the oil – if it sizzles, it's ready.

4 Fry the squid in batches, a few at a time, for 2–3 minutes until crisp and golden brown. Remove with a slotted spoon and drain on kitchen paper. Take care not to overcook them or they will become rubbery.

5 Serve piping hot, sprinkled with salt, with lemon wedges for squeezing.

Tip: An easy way to coat the squid is to shake it with the seasoned flour in a ziplock bag.

VARIATION
Add some ground paprika or dried oregano to the flour.

SOUVLAKI & GYROS

ΣΟΥΒΛΑΚΙ & ΓΥΡΟΣ

CHICKEN SOUVLAKI

KOTOPOULO SOUVLAKI

SERVES 4
PREP: 10 MINUTES
MARINATE: 30 MINUTES
COOK: 8–10 MINUTES

900g/2lb skinned, boned chicken breasts, cut into cubes

4 pita breads (see page 11)

4–8 tbsp souvlaki sauce (see page 10)

a few crisp Cos (romaine) lettuce leaves, shredded

3 ripe tomatoes, sliced or coarsely chopped

1 small red onion, thinly sliced

oregano potato fries (see page 98) or French fries

chopped flat-leaf (Italian) parsley, for sprinkling

smoked paprika, for dusting

Make these delicious souvlaki and eat like a real Athenian. You can serve them wrapped in warm pita, as suggested below, or on the skewers on a serving platter and help yourself to salad, fries, pita and dips. It's up to you!

1 To make the marinade, combine all the ingredients together in a bowl until well blended.

2 Thread the chicken cubes on to 12 short or 8 long bamboo skewers and place them in a shallow bowl. Spoon the marinade over them and set aside in a cool place or the fridge for 30 minutes, turning them occasionally.

3 Preheat the barbecue or an overhead grill (broiler) to high. Cook the chicken skewers for 8–10 minutes, turning occasionally, until cooked through and golden brown all over. Alternatively, cook them in a ridged griddle (grill) pan over a high heat. Don't overcook them or they will become tough and dry.

MARINADE:
2 garlic cloves, crushed
1 tsp dried oregano
1 tsp dried thyme
grated zest and juice of
   1 lemon
5 tbsp olive oil
sea salt and freshly ground
   black pepper

4 Warm the pita breads in the oven or on a hot griddle pan. Spread a little souvlaki sauce over each one and top with the lettuce, tomato and onion.

5 Remove the chicken from the skewers and arrange on top with the oregano potato fries or French fries. Sprinkle with parsley and dust with smoked paprika, then fold the pitas over and around the filling and roll up in some baking parchment or kitchen foil (aluminum foil) to hold the filling in place. Enjoy!

Tip: Soak the bamboo skewers in water for 30 minutes to prevent them scorching.

VARIATIONS
• Substitute tzatziki (see page 24) or yoghurt sauce (see page 8) for the souvlaki sauce.
• Add some griddled sliced halloumi.

HALLOUMI SOUVLAKI

SERVES 4
PREP: 15 MINUTES
COOK: 8–12
MINUTES

1 tbsp olive oil
500g/1lb 2oz halloumi, sliced
2 tsp dried oregano
4 pita breads (see page 11)
4–8 tbsp tzatziki (see page 24)
a few crisp lettuce leaves, e.g. Cos (romaine), shredded
3 ripe tomatoes, sliced or coarsely chopped
1 small red onion, thinly sliced
oregano potato fries (see page 98) or French fries
sea salt and freshly ground black pepper
chopped flat-leaf (Italian) parsley, for sprinkling
smoked paprika, for dusting

When you want a tasty plant-based souvlaki, this is the perfect solution. Vegans can substitute non-dairy vegan tzatziki (see page 24) and vegan halloumi for the traditional Greek ones.

1 Heat the oil in a large frying pan (skillet) or ridged griddle (grill) pan set over a medium heat. When the pan is hot, cook the halloumi in batches for 2–3 minutes on each side until crisp and golden and starting to soften inside. Do not overcook or it will be charred and rubbery. Remove and drain on kitchen paper (paper towels). Sprinkle with the oregano.

2 Warm the pita breads in the oven or on a hot griddle pan. Spread the tzatziki over each one and top with the lettuce, tomato and onion.

3 Arrange the halloumi on top with the oregano potato fries or French fries. Season with salt and pepper, sprinkle with parsley and dust with smoked paprika.

4 Fold the pitas over and around the filling and roll up in some baking parchment or kitchen foil (aluminum foil) to hold the filling in place. Enjoy!

Tip: The halloumi tastes fabulous if you cook it over hot coals on a barbecue. Place on the oiled grill and cook for 2 minutes on each side until golden brown.

VARIATIONS
- Dust the halloumi with a little flour before cooking for a crispier coating.
- Drizzle with hot sauce or pomegranate molasses.
- Use Talagani cheese instead of halloumi.

PORK SOUVLAKI

HIRINO SOUVLAKI

SERVES 4
PREP: 15 MINUTES
MARINATE: 2 HOURS
OR OVERNIGHT
COOK: 10 MINUTES

800g/1lb 12oz lean pork fillet (tenderloin), cut into cubes
4 pita breads (see page 11)
4 tbsp souvlaki sauce (see page 10)
a few crisp Cos (romaine) lettuce leaves, shredded
3 ripe tomatoes, sliced or coarsely chopped
1 small red onion, thinly sliced
4 tbsp tzatziki (see page 24)
oregano potato fries (see page 98) or French fries
chopped flat-leaf (Italian) parsley, for sprinkling
smoked paprika, for dusting

Tender pork souvlaki are very popular in Greece and an Athenian speciality. They couldn't be easier to make, so why not have a go and treat yourself? For more colour and flavour, add some chunks of green or yellow (bell) pepper and onion to the pork skewers.

1 To make the marinade, mix all the ingredients together in a bowl until well combined.

2 Thread the pork on to 12 short or 8 long bamboo skewers and place them in a shallow bowl. Spoon the marinade over them, then cover and chill in the fridge for 2 hours, turning them occasionally. Or, for a more intense flavour, leave them overnight.

3 Preheat the barbecue or an overhead grill (broiler) to high. Cook the pork skewers for 8–10 minutes, turning occasionally, until cooked through, tender and golden brown all over. Alternatively, cook them in a ridged griddle (grill) pan over a high heat.

4 Warm the pita breads in the oven or on a hot griddle pan. Spread a little souvlaki sauce over each one and top with the lettuce, tomato and onion.

5 Remove the pork from the skewers and arrange on top with the tzatziki and oregano potato fries or French fries. Sprinkle with parsley and dust with smoked paprika, then fold the pitas around the filling and roll up in some baking parchment or kitchen foil (aluminum foil) to hold the filling in place. Enjoy!

MARINADE:

2 garlic cloves, crushed
2 tsp dried oregano
1 tsp ground cumin
1 tsp ground coriander
1 tsp smoked paprika
6 tbsp olive oil
sea salt and freshly ground
    black pepper

VARIATIONS
- Add some lemon juice to the marinade to make the pork more tender.
- Instead of wrapping the pork and salad in the pita breads, serve deconstructed on a platter for people to help themselves.

Tip: Soak the bamboo skewers in water for 30 minutes to prevent them scorching.

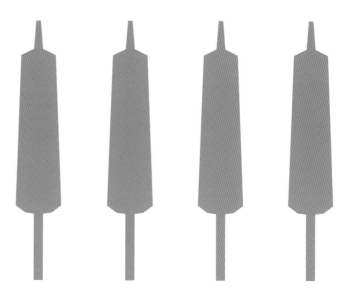

PORK GYROS

GYROS HIRINO

SERVES 4
PREP: 20 MINUTES
MARINATE: 2 HOURS
OR OVERNIGHT
COOK: 4 HOURS

6 thin slices of pork
 shoulder
6 thin slices of pancetta
½ white onion
4 pita breads (see page 11)
8–12 tbsp tzatziki (see
 page 24)
a few crisp Cos (romaine)
 lettuce leaves, shredded
4 ripe tomatoes, sliced or
 coarsely chopped
1 medium red onion,
 thinly sliced
oregano potato fries (see
 page 98) or French fries
chopped flat-leaf (Italian)
 parsley, for sprinkling
smoked paprika, for
 dusting

Slow-cooking the meat in the oven for several hours on a very low heat is well worth the effort as it makes the pork extremely tender, juicy and succulent. If you cook it more quickly at a higher heat it will become dry and chewy.

1 Mix all the marinade ingredients together in a bowl until well combined.

2 Dip each slice of pork into the marinade to cover both sides. Remove and dip each slice of pancetta into the marinade.

3 Take a slice of the marinated pork and cover with a slice of pancetta. Continue layering up alternately in this way, finishing with a slice of pancetta. Place the stack in a clean bowl and pour the remaining marinade over the top. Cover and chill in the fridge for at least 2 hours or, better still, overnight.

4 When you're ready to cook the meat, preheat the oven to 130°C/250°F/gas mark ½.

5 Remove the stack of pork and pancetta from the marinade and place on a baking tray. Place the onion half on top and secure with 4 bamboo or wooden skewers, inserting them through the onion and all the meat layers. Cook in the oven for 4 hours until the pork is meltingly tender.

MARINADE:
2 garlic cloves, crushed
1 tsp dried oregano
1 tsp ground cumin
1 tsp smoked paprika
1 tsp ground coriander
1 tsp ground black pepper
2 tsp sea salt
10 tbsp olive oil

6 When the pork is cooked, place the stack on a board and slice down through it very thinly with a sharp knife to 'shave' the meat.

7 Warm the pita breads in the oven or on a hot griddle (grill) pan. Spread the tzatziki over them and pile the sliced meat on top.

8 Add the lettuce, tomato and sliced onion together with the oregano potato fries or French fries. Sprinkle with parsley and dust with smoked paprika, then fold the pitas around the filling and roll up in some baking parchment or kitchen foil (aluminum foil) to hold the filling in place. Enjoy!

> **Tip: By cutting down as thinly as you can through the cooked pork and pancetta stack, you can achieve a similar effect to the thinly sliced meat for gyros that is cooked on a vertical rotisserie.**

> **VARIATIONS**
> • Add some souvlaki sauce (see page 10) to the gyros.
> • Tuck in some fried or griddled sliced halloumi if you're feeling very hungry.
> • Crumble some feta over the pork.

VEGAN SEITAN GYROS

SERVES 4
PREP: 20 MINUTES
COOK: 30 MINUTES

500g/1lb 2oz seitan, cut into thin strips
4 pita breads (see page 11)
250g/9oz (1 cup) vegan tzatziki (see page 24)
a few crisp Cos (romaine) lettuce leaves, shredded
4 ripe tomatoes, sliced or coarsely chopped
1 medium red onion, thinly sliced
oregano potato fries (see page 98) or French fries
chopped flat-leaf (Italian) parsley, for sprinkling
smoked paprika, for dusting

MARINADE:
1 garlic clove, crushed
½ tsp grated lemon zest
1 tsp dried oregano
1 tsp dried thyme
1 tsp ground cumin
1 tsp ground coriander
½ tsp smoked paprika
½ tsp cayenne pepper
½ tsp freshly ground black pepper
½ tsp sea salt
juice of 1 lemon
5 tbsp olive oil
240ml/8fl oz (1 cup) water

Plant-based gyros are becoming all the rage as more people embrace vegan food, and not just in Veganuary! These seitan ones are high in protein and among our favourites. Serve them in a pita wrap or deconstructed on a plate with warm pita triangles.

1 Preheat the oven to 200°C/400°F/gas mark 6.

2 To make the marinade, mix all the ingredients together in a bowl. When they are well combined, add the seitan and stir well. Set aside for 5 minutes to allow the seitan to absorb the flavours of the marinade.

3 Transfer to an ovenproof dish or roasting pan and cook in the preheated oven for 30 minutes, or until the seitan is golden brown and crispy on top.

4 Serve deconstructed with warm pita breads, vegan tzatziki, lettuce, tomato, onion and oregano potato fries or French fries, sprinkled with parsley and paprika. Alternatively, generously smear the warm pita breads with tzatziki and load with the seitan, salad and fries to eat as a wrap.

VARIATIONS
• Serve the crispy seitan with a leafy green salad and tzatziki with some warm pita.
• Instead of using seitan, make vegan gyros with crispy fried tofu or vegan halloumi.

CHICKEN GYROS

GYROS KOTOPOULO

SERVES 4
PREP: 20 MINUTES
MARINATE: 2 HOURS
OR OVERNIGHT
COOK: 3 HOURS

4 boned, skinless chicken
thighs
1 boned chicken thigh, skin on
½ white onion
4 pita breads (see page 11)
8–12 tbsp tzatziki (see
page 24)
a few crisp Cos (romaine)
lettuce leaves, shredded
4 ripe tomatoes, sliced or
coarsely chopped
1 medium red onion, thinly
sliced
oregano potato fries (see
page 98) or French fries
chopped flat-leaf (Italian)
parsley, for sprinkling
smoked paprika, for
dusting

MARINADE:
2 garlic cloves, crushed
1 tsp dried oregano
1 tsp smoked paprika
1 tsp freshly ground black
pepper
½ tbsp sea salt
½ tsp ground cumin
½ tsp ground coriander
½ tsp grated lemon zest
juice of 2 lemons
2 tbsp olive oil

Traditionally, the meat for gyros is cooked on a vertical rotisserie and then carved very thinly before adding to warm pita with sauce, fries and salad. It's easy to recreate this at home if you follow our recipe. Although it takes a while to cook, the hands-on time is minimal.

1 Mix all the marinade ingredients together in a bowl until well combined. Add the chicken thighs, turning them in the marinade. Cover the bowl and leave to marinate in the fridge for at least 2 hours or, better still, overnight.

2 When you're ready to cook the chicken, preheat the oven to 130°C/250°F/gas mark ½.

3 Remove the chicken from the marinade and place the skinless thighs on top of each other in a stack. Cover with the remaining chicken thigh, skin-side up, and then place the onion half on top. Secure with 4 bamboo or wooden skewers, inserting them through the onion and all the chicken layers. Transfer to a baking tray and cook in the oven for 3 hours until the chicken is very tender.

4 When the chicken is cooked, place the stack on a board and, with the skewers in place to secure the meat, slice down through it very thinly with a sharp knife to 'shave' it and create the gyros effect.

Continued overleaf →

5 Warm the pita breads in the oven or on a hot griddle (grill) pan. Spread the tzatziki over them and pile the sliced chicken on top.

6 Add the lettuce, tomato and onion together with the oregano potato fries or French fries. Sprinkle with parsley and dust with smoked paprika, then fold the pitas around the filling and roll up in some baking parchment or kitchen foil (aluminum foil) to hold the filling in place.

7 Alternatively, arrange the shaved chicken, warm pita breads and fries on a serving board or platter with a bowl of tzatziki and another of tomato, red onion and lettuce. Sprinkle with parsley, dust with smoked paprika and serve, allowing people to help themselves.

VARIATIONS
- Use souvlaki sauce (see page 10) instead of tzatziki.
- Add some crushed chilli flakes to the marinade.
- Sprinkle the cooked chicken with dried oregano before serving.

Tip: If you're in a hurry, you can cook the chicken at 170°C/325°F/gas mark 3 for 2 hours, although it will not be so tender. The longer it's cooked, the softer it gets.

LIGHT MEALS, BREAKFASTS & BRUNCHES

ΜΙΚΡΑ ΓΕΥΜΑΤΑ, ΠΡΩΙΝΟ & ΜΠΡΑΝΤΣ

GREEK FRITTATA

FROUTALIA

3 tbsp olive oil
3 medium courgettes
   (zucchini), thinly sliced
3 garlic cloves, crushed
4 ripe tomatoes, chopped
150g/5oz spinach, washed
   and roughly chopped
8 medium free-range eggs
a few sprigs of dill, finely
   chopped
85g/3oz feta, crumbled
sea salt and freshly ground
   black pepper

This Greek twist on an Italian frittata makes a delicious breakfast, brunch or light supper dish. It's best eaten lukewarm rather than piping hot, but it also tastes good served cold for a packed lunch or picnic.

1 Heat 2 tablespoons of the oil in a large frying pan (skillet) set over a medium heat. Add the courgettes and cook, turning occasionally, for 5 minutes until tender and golden. Add the garlic and tomatoes and cook for 2–3 minutes. Stir in the spinach and cook for 1 minute until it wilts and turns bright green.

2 Beat the eggs in a large bowl and season with salt and pepper. Stir in the courgette mixture and dill.

3 Heat the remaining oil in the pan and pour in the egg mixture. Sprinkle the feta over the top and cook gently over a low heat for 8–10 minutes, or until the frittata is set and golden underneath and only the top is still runny.

4 Flash the pan under a preheated overhead grill (broiler) for 2–3 minutes, or until the top of the frittata is set and golden brown.

5 Slide the frittata out of the pan on to a board and cut into 4 wedges. Serve lukewarm or cold.

VARIATIONS
- Instead of feta, use some grated Graviera cheese.
- If wished, substitute chopped flat-leaf (Italian) parsley or Greek basil for the dill.
- Add some sliced spring onions (scallions), Greek salami or sausage.

GREEK BREAKFAST MUFFINS

MAKES 12
PREP: 15 MINUTES
COOK: 30 MINUTES

2 tbsp olive oil, plus extra
  for greasing
1 red onion, chopped
150g/5oz baby spinach
  leaves, coarsely chopped
a few sprigs of flat-leaf
  (Italian) parsley, chopped
250g/9oz (2½ cups) self-
  raising (self-rising) flour
1 tsp bicarbonate of soda
  (baking soda)
a pinch of salt
2 medium free-range eggs
225g/8oz (generous 1 cup)
  Greek yoghurt
100g/3½oz (1 cup) grated
  Graviera or Kefalotyri
  cheese, plus extra for
  sprinkling
2 large carrots, grated
3 tbsp mixed seeds,
  e.g. poppy, sunflower,
  pumpkin

Grab one of these delicious healthy muffins for a quick breakfast or to eat on-the-go. They are also great for a mid-morning snack or to pop into a lunchbox.

1 Preheat the oven to 200°C/400°F/gas mark 6. Line a 12-hole muffin pan with paper cases (liners).

2 Heat the oil in a pan set over a medium heat and cook the onion, stirring occasionally, for 6–8 minutes, or until tender. Add the spinach and cook for 1 minute until the leaves wilt. Stir in the parsley and set aside to cool.

3 Sift the flour, bicarbonate of soda and salt into a large bowl. Beat the eggs and yoghurt and stir into the flour with the cooled onion and spinach mixture. Gently fold in the cheese, grated carrot and seeds, taking care not to over-mix.

4 Divide the mixture between the paper cases and sprinkle lightly with grated cheese. Bake in the preheated oven for 18–20 minutes, or until the muffins are risen and golden brown. To test whether they are cooked, insert a thin skewer into the centre – it should come out clean.

5 Remove the muffins from the pan and cool on a wire rack. Eat warm or at room temperature. They will keep well in a sealed container for 2 days or in a sealed bag in the freezer for up to 1 month.

VARIATIONS
- If you can't find Graviera cheese, use Cheddar instead.
- Substitute snipped chives or dill for the parsley.
- Flavour with crushed garlic or grated nutmeg.
- Add some pine nuts or chopped walnuts.

GREEK PIZZAS

SERVES 4
PREP: 15 MINUTES
COOK: 15–20
MINUTES

1 quantity pita bread
    dough (see page 11)
4 juicy tomatoes, chopped
    or grated
olive oil, for drizzling
a good pinch of dried
    oregano
200g/7oz (2 cups) grated
    Graviera cheese
1 large green (bell) pepper,
    deseeded and thinly sliced
100g/3½oz feta
sea salt and freshly ground
    black pepper
fresh basil leaves, for
    sprinkling

These individual pizzas are so easy to make when you're you're in a hurry, or you can use ready-made pitas rather than making the dough yourself. They're perfect for a tasty snack when you're feeling peckish, or for a light lunch.

1 Preheat the oven to 170°C/325°F/gas mark 3.

2 Make 4 pitas with the pita bread dough (see page 11) and place on 2 baking trays.

3 Spread the tomatoes over the top of each pita, leaving a 1 cm border around the edge. Drizzle with olive oil, sprinkle lightly with oregano and season with salt and pepper. Cover with the grated cheese and add the sliced green pepper. Crumble the feta over the top.

4 Bake in the preheated oven for 15–20 minutes, or until the cheese melts and the pizza bases are crisp and golden.

5 Cut each pizza into quarters and serve hot, sprinkled with basil leaves.

VEGAN PIZZAS

Substitute Violife slices and mozzarella-flavour plant-based 'cheese' for the Graviera and feta.

Note: You can buy 'raw' ready-to-cook pita breads from The Athenian.

VARIATIONS
- Use grated Kefalotyri, Cheddar or mozzarella instead of Graviera.
- Use a red or yellow (bell) pepper instead of a green one.

BREAKFAST MEAL IN A BOWL

SERVES 4
PREP: 10 MINUTES
COOK: 1 HOUR

5 tbsp olive oil, plus extra for brushing

a few drops of balsamic vinegar

a few sprigs of fresh rosemary and thyme

450g/1lb cherry or baby plum tomatoes, halved

300g/10oz spinach, washed, trimmed and roughly chopped

250g/9oz mushrooms, left whole, halved or quartered

3 garlic cloves, crushed

250g/9oz halloumi, sliced

4 medium free-range eggs

sea salt and freshly ground black pepper

chopped flat-leaf (Italian) parsley or chives, for sprinkling

toasted pita or flatbreads (see page 11), to serve

Note: Vegans can omit the eggs and substitute vegan non-dairy halloumi or sliced tofu for the halloumi.

This vegetarian meal in a bowl is so colourful, healthy and delicious. It's great to start the day or to serve for a weekend brunch. Slow-cooking the tomatoes in this way is well worth the effort as it gives them an intensely sweet flavour.

1 Preheat the oven to 150°C/300°F/gas mark 2.

2 Mix together 2 tablespoons of the olive oil, the balsamic vinegar and herbs. Pour over a baking tray and place the tomatoes on top, cut-side down. Season with salt and pepper and cook in the preheated oven for 1 hour, or until they are softened and starting to wrinkle.

3 About 15–20 minutes before the tomatoes are ready, put the spinach in a colander and pour over 2–3 kettles of boiling water until it really wilts and softens. Press down firmly with a saucer to extract all the moisture and then chop and set aside.

4 Fry the mushrooms and garlic in the remaining olive oil in a large frying pan (skillet) set over a medium heat for 6–8 minutes until tender and golden brown. Season to taste with salt and pepper, remove and keep warm.

5 Brush a ridged griddle (grill) pan with oil and set over a medium heat. When it's hot, add the halloumi and cook, in batches, for 2–3 minutes on each side until tender, golden brown and attractively striped. Don't overcook or it will become rubbery. Remove from the pan and keep warm.

6 Meanwhile, set a large pan of water over a high heat. As soon as it starts to boil, reduce the heat to medium and carefully add the eggs, using a slotted spoon. Cook in the bubbling water for 6–7 minutes (until the whites are set but the yolks are still runny) and then remove with a slotted spoon.

7 Plunge the eggs into a bowl of iced water and leave for 2 minutes until they are cool enough for you to gently peel away the shell.

8 Arrange the spinach, mushrooms, tomatoes and halloumi in 4 shallow bowls. Nestle an egg in the centre of each bowl and season lightly with salt and pepper. Sprinkle with chopped herbs and serve immediately with toasted pita or flatbreads.

> **Tip: If wished, you can squash the eggs gently with a fork to break them open so the yolks run out over the spinach and mushrooms.**

VARIATIONS
- Instead of halloumi, crumble some feta over the top.
- Use poached eggs instead of soft-boiled.
- If you're in a hurry, just grill (broil) or fry the tomatoes.

EGG & HALLOUMI BREAKFAST SANDWICH

SERVES 2
PREP: 5 MINUTES
COOK: 10–15 MINUTES

2 tbsp olive oil
125g/4½oz halloumi cheese, cut into 4 slices
2 tomatoes, halved
2 medium free-range eggs
2 burger buns or bread rolls
2 tbsp mayonnaise (optional)
sea salt and freshly ground black pepper
tomato ketchup or hot sauce, to serve

This toasted sandwich is very filling and will energize you ahead of a busy day. The great thing about halloumi is its high melting point, making it perfect for frying, grilling (broiling) and even barbecuing. We've used bread rolls, but you could go full-on Greek and substitute pita breads or just roll up the filling in a wrap.

1 Heat 1 tablespoon of the oil in a non-stick frying pan (skillet) set over a medium heat. Add the halloumi and cook for 2–3 minutes until golden brown and crispy underneath. Turn the slices over and cook on the other side for 2–3 minutes until browned. Remove from the pan and keep warm.

2 Add the tomatoes to the pan, cut-side down, and fry for 2–3 minutes, just long enough to heat and soften them. Remove and set aside.

3 Add the remaining tablespoon of oil to the pan and fry the eggs for 3–4 minutes, or until the whites are set and the yolks are still a little runny.

4 Meanwhile, cut the buns or rolls in half and lightly toast them.

5 Spread the mayonnaise (if using) over the bottom half of each bun and cover with the tomatoes. Next, add the sliced halloumi and top each one with a fried egg. Season lightly with salt and pepper, and cover with the top halves of the buns.

6 Serve immediately with some tomato ketchup or hot sauce on the side.

VARIATIONS
- Add some lettuce, rocket (arugula) or baby spinach leaves.
- Sprinkle the egg with freshly chopped basil, chives or dill, or a pinch of dried oregano.
- Add some fried mushrooms or crispy bacon.

BEEF BURGERS

BIFTEKI

SERVES 4
PREP: 15 MINUTES
CHILL: 15 MINUTES
COOK: 30 MINUTES

1 small red onion, grated
1 garlic clove, crushed
500g/1lb 2oz (2¼ cups)
   minced (ground) beef
45g/1½oz (scant 1 cup)
   fresh white breadcrumbs
1 medium free-range egg,
   beaten
a handful of flat-leaf
   (Italian) parsley, chopped
½ tsp dried oregano
1 tbsp olive oil, plus extra
   for brushing
1 tbsp red wine vinegar
1 tsp sea salt
freshly ground black
   pepper
fried, mashed or baked
   potatoes, to serve

TOPPINGS (optional):
sliced tomato
sliced feta
cheese slices

These juicy succulent beef patties are served throughout Greece all the year round. For the best flavour use good-quality beef (not too fat nor too lean) and make them by hand, squashing and kneading the ingredients together to bring out the flavour of the herbs and seasonings. You can also cook them over hot coals on a barbecue, under a grill (broiler) or in a griddle (grill) pan. In Greece they are not usually eaten in a bun.

1 Preheat the oven to 190°C/375°F/gas mark 5. Line a baking tray with baking parchment.

2 Put all the ingredients in a bowl and, using your hands, mix and gently squeeze them together to form a ball. If it's too damp and sticky, mix in some more breadcrumbs; if it's too dry, add a little water or some milk.

3 Cover the bowl and chill in the fridge for at least 15 minutes to firm up the mixture.

4 Divide the mixture into 4 equal-sized portions and shape each one into a patty. Place them on the lined baking tray and brush lightly with oil.

5 Cook in the preheated oven for 25–30 minutes, turning them halfway through, until thoroughly cooked. Serve plain, or topped with sliced tomato, feta or cheese, with a squeeze of lemon.

Tip: If you don't want to mix everything by hand in the traditional way, use a food mixer.

VARIATIONS
• Add some chopped green fennel fronds or mint to the beef mixture.
• For a spicy option, add some ground cumin or paprika.

GREEK CLUB SANDWICH

1 tbsp olive oil
2 x 85g/3oz thin skinless chicken breast fillets
1 garlic clove, crushed
4 rashers (slices) of streaky bacon
6 slices of wholegrain or multi-seed bread
8 tbsp tzatziki (see page 24)
¼ Cos (romaine) lettuce, shredded
2 juicy tomatoes, sliced
2 thin slices of feta
sea salt and freshly ground black pepper
hot sauce or tomato ketchup, to serve

Who doesn't love a club sandwich? The Greeks are no exception and it's become a popular beach snack or light lunch. We've layered ours with tzatziki, but you could be more traditional and use mayonnaise instead. For a vegetarian version, omit the chicken and bacon in favour of grilled (broiled) vegetables, such as mushrooms, aubergine (eggplant) and courgettes (zucchini).

1 Heat the olive oil in a frying pan (skillet) set over a medium heat. When it's hot, add the chicken breast fillets and cook for 5–6 minutes on each side or until golden brown and cooked right through. Add the crushed garlic for the last 2–3 minutes to flavour them. Remove from the pan and set aside to cool.

2 Cook the bacon in the pan for 2 minutes on each side, or until golden brown and crispy. Remove and drain on kitchen paper (paper towels).

3 Lightly toast the bread and brush lightly with the oil left in the pan.

4 Place a slice of toasted bread on a board and spread with a little tzatziki (about 1 tablespoon). Cover with half of the lettuce and tomatoes and top with 2 bacon rashers.

Continued overleaf →

5 Spread some tzatziki over another slice of toast and place, tzatziki-side down, on top. Lightly spread the toast with some more tzatziki and cover with a slice of feta. Don't worry if it breaks – just crumble it over the tzatziki.

6 Thinly slice the chicken, season lightly with salt and pepper and place half of it on top of the feta. Spread some more tzatziki over a piece of toast and place on top, tzatziki-side down.

7 Secure the sandwich with wooden cocktail sticks (toothpicks) and cut diagonally into 2 halves, or into quarters. Repeat with the remaining toasted bread slices and filling, assembling them in the same way. Serve immediately with hot sauce or tomato ketchup.

VARIATIONS
- Substitute baby spinach leaves for the lettuce.
- Add some thinly sliced red onion or chopped spring onions (scallions).
- Try sliced Graviera or grilled halloumi instead of feta.
- Add some thinly sliced ham.

Tip: If the chicken breasts are thick, flatten them out before cooking, bashing them with a rolling pin or meat mallet to make them thinner.

MEATBALLS

KEFTEDAKIA

SERVES 4
PREP: 15 MINUTES
CHILL: 30 MINUTES
COOK: 15–20 MINUTES

115g/4oz white bread, crusts removed
500g/1lb 2oz (2¼ cups) minced (ground) beef
1 onion, grated
1 garlic clove, crushed
1 tsp dried oregano
a few sprigs of flat-leaf (Italian) parsley, chopped
a few sprigs of mint, chopped
1 tsp sea salt
freshly ground black pepper
2 medium free-range eggs, beaten
2 tbsp olive oil
a dash of red wine vinegar
plain (all-purpose) flour, for dusting
vegetable oil, for deep-frying

TO SERVE:
chopped flat-leaf (Italian) parsley
lemon quarters
tomatoes and sliced red onions
tzatziki or yoghurt sauce (see pages 24 and 8)

These little meatballs are so tasty and quick and easy to make. They are very versatile, too, as you can eat them freshly cooked as a snack or canapé, wrap them in pita bread or tortillas, or add them to a tomato sauce and toss them with pasta.

1 Put the bread in a small bowl and pour a little cold water over it. Set aside until the bread soaks up the water. Squeeze out any excess water with your hands and discard.

2 Transfer the bread to a large bowl and add the beef, onion, garlic, herbs, salt and pepper, eggs, oil and vinegar. Stir well, mixing until everything is well combined – use your hands, if preferred, to draw the mixture together. If the mixture seems too dry, add a little water to moisten it; if it's too sloppy, add some more bread.

3 Cover the bowl and chill in the fridge for at least 30 minutes. This will allow the mixture to rest and firm up.

4 Divide the mixture into 20 portions and, using your hands, shape each one into a ball. Lightly dust the balls with flour.

5 Heat the vegetable oil in a deep-fryer or, if you don't have one, half-fill a large heavy pan with oil. Deep-fry the meatballs, in batches, for 4–5 minutes until golden brown all over. Remove with a slotted spoon and drain on kitchen paper (paper towels).

6 Serve immediately, sprinkled with parsley, with lemons for squeezing and a garnish of tomatoes and sliced red onions. Serve with tzatziki or yoghurt sauce.

VARIATIONS
• Wrap the meatballs with some lettuce, tomatoes, red onion and oregano fries in pita breads, souvlaki-style.

LENTIL SOUP

FAKES SOUPA

SERVES 4–6
PREP: 10 MINUTES
COOK: 50 MINUTES

2 tbsp olive oil, plus extra
for drizzling
2 red onions, chopped
3 garlic cloves, crushed
450g/1lb (generous 2 cups)
brown lentils (dry weight)
1 litre/1¾ pints (generous
4 cups) vegetable stock
2 bay leaves
1 sprig of rosemary
1 tbsp tomato paste
200g/7oz (1 cup) canned
chopped tomatoes in
their juice
½ tsp ground cinnamon
1–2 tbsp red wine vinegar,
plus extra to serve
sea salt and freshly ground
black pepper
crumbled feta cheese, for
sprinkling (optional)

Use the small Greek brown lentils in this traditional comfort soup to obtain the best and most authentic texture and flavour. Small green lentils will also work well but avoid the red Syrian ones, which break down and go mushy. The soup is also sometimes made without the tomato paste and tomatoes, so you can omit them if you like.

1 Heat the olive oil in a large saucepan set over a medium heat. Cook the onions, stirring occasionally, for 6–8 minutes, or until softened. Add the garlic and cook for 2 minutes without colouring.

2 Meanwhile, put the lentils in another saucepan and cover with cold water. Set over a high heat and bring to the boil, then drain in a sieve.

3 Add the lentils to the onions and garlic, together with the vegetable stock and herbs. Stir in the tomato paste and tomatoes and bring to the boil. Reduce the heat to low and simmer gently for 40 minutes, or until the lentils are tender and the soup thickens. Stir in 1 tablespoon of red wine vinegar and season to taste with salt and pepper. If wished, add another spoonful of vinegar. Remove and discard the herbs.

4 Ladle the soup into bowls and serve drizzled with olive oil. If liked, crumble some feta over the top. Place some red wine vinegar on the table for people to help themselves.

Tip: Although lentils do not require soaking you should rinse them under running cold water before using them. Pick them over to remove any tiny stones and pieces of grit before cooking.

VARIATIONS
- Add some chopped spinach leaves for the last 5 minutes, or stir in some lemon juice.
- Sprinkle with chopped flat-leaf (Italian) parsley.

CHICKPEA BURGERS

REVITHOKEFTEDES

SERVES 4
PREP: 15 MINUTES
CHILL: 15 MINUTES
COOK: 8–10 MINUTES

400g/14oz (1½ cups)
  canned chickpeas
  (garbanzo beans), rinsed
  and drained
½ red onion, chopped
3 garlic cloves
a handful of flat-leaf
  (Italian) parsley
½ tsp ground cumin
½ tsp paprika
grated zest and juice of
  1 lemon
1 medium free-range egg
100g/3½oz (2 cups) fresh
  white breadcrumbs
vegetable oil, for frying
sea salt and freshly ground
  black pepper

**Note: We've used
canned chickpeas for
speed and convenience,
but you can soak
and cook some dried
chickpeas before
blitzing with the
other ingredients.**

**You can eat these delicious veggie burgers with some salad
and fried potatoes or serve them in a bun or wrapped in a
soft fluffy pita bread. The mixture is very versatile and you
can also shape it into small balls and serve them fried as an
appetizer or *meze* dish. You could make double the quantity
and freeze some uncooked burgers – they will keep for up
to 1 month in the freezer.**

1 Blitz the chickpeas, onion, garlic, parsley, spices, lemon
zest and juice, and egg in a food processor until coarsely
chopped and well combined. Stop before it becomes
smooth – you want some texture.

2 Transfer to a bowl and mix in three-quarters of the
breadcrumbs and seasoning to taste. If the mixture
seems too damp, stir in some more breadcrumbs or
a little flour; if it's too dry, add some more beaten egg
or lemon juice. Cover and chill in the fridge for at least
15 minutes to firm up.

3 Divide the mixture into 4 equal-sized pieces and shape
each one into a burger. Coat lightly with the remaining
breadcrumbs.

4 Heat the oil in a large frying pan (skillet) set over a
medium heat. Add the burgers and cook for 4–5 minutes
on each side, turning them carefully, until crisp and golden
brown. Remove from the pan and drain on kitchen paper
(paper towels).

5 If wished, serve in burger buns or pita breads with some
lettuce, tomatoes and red onion, drizzled with tzatziki or
yoghurt sauce.

TO SERVE (optional):
4 burger buns or pita
   breads (see page 11)
shredded lettuce, sliced
   tomatoes and red onion
tzatziki or yoghurt sauce
   (see pages 24 and 8)

**Tip: You can just dust
the burgers with flour
rather than coating
them with breadcrumbs.**

VEGAN BURGERS

Omit the egg and fry
the onion and garlic in
olive oil until softened
before blitzing them
in the food processor.
Serve with vegan
tzatziki (see page 24).

VARIATIONS
- Substitute coriander (cilantro) for the parsley.
- Add a diced red or green chilli for some heat.
- Serve drizzled with hot sauce.

MUM'S HOME RECIPES

ΣΥΝΤΑΓΕΣ ΤΗΣ ΜΑΜΑΣ

WHITE BEAN SOUP

FASOLADA

SERVES 4
PREP: 15 MINUTES
SOAK: OVERNIGHT
COOK: 1½ HOURS

500g/1lb 2oz (2½ cups)
　white beans, e.g.
　cannellini or haricot
　(navy) beans (dry weight)
4 tbsp olive oil
1 large onion, chopped
2 carrots, finely chopped
2 celery sticks, diced
3 garlic cloves, crushed
1 litre/1¾ pints (generous
　4 cups) vegetable stock
1 bay leaf
2 sprigs of thyme, leaves
　picked
juice of 1 lemon
a handful of flat-leaf
　(Italian) parsley, chopped
sea salt and freshly ground
　black pepper
crusty bread, to serve

This soup will warm you up on a cold winter's day, but in Greece it's also eaten in summer. It's important to use soaked dried beans and not canned for the best and most authentic flavour and texture. It freezes well, so why not make double the quantity and freeze a batch to thaw and reheat when you're in a hurry and don't have time to cook?

1 Soak the beans overnight in a bowl of cold water. The following day, drain well and transfer the beans to a large saucepan. Cover with plenty of fresh cold water and bring to the boil. Reduce the heat to low and cook for about 40 minutes, or until just tender but not mushy. Drain well.

2 Heat the olive oil in a large saucepan set over a medium heat. Add the onion, carrots, celery and garlic and cook, stirring occasionally, for 6–8 minutes, or until softened.

3 Add the vegetable stock, herbs, lemon juice and cooked beans, and bring to the boil. Reduce the heat to a simmer and cook gently for 35–40 minutes, or until the beans are cooked and the vegetables are tender.

4 Discard the bay leaf and blitz half of the soup in a blender or food processor until smooth. Return to the pan and stir in the parsley. Season to taste with salt and pepper.

5 Serve immediately, sprinkled with parsley and some crusty bread on the side, or with crumbled feta cheese and crusty bread.

VARIATIONS
- Add some chopped fresh spinach to the soup after blending and cook for an additional 5 minutes.

SPINACH & FETA PIE

SPANAKOPITA

SERVES 6
PREP: 20 MINUTES
COOK: 45–50
MINUTES

4 tbsp olive oil, plus extra
   for brushing
1.5kg/3lb spinach, washed
   and trimmed
2 bunches of spring onions
   (scallions), finely chopped
2 garlic cloves, crushed
1 small bunch of dill, finely
   chopped
300g/10oz feta, crumbled
100g/3½oz (1 cup) grated
   Kefalotyri or Graviera
   cheese
grated zest of 1 lemon
½ tsp freshly grated
   nutmeg
2 medium free-range eggs,
   beaten
300g/10oz pack (or 12
   -sheets) filo (phyllo) pastry
freshly grated black pepper

**This healthy spinach pie is as Greek as it gets! And the
good news is that it's packed with vitamins and minerals,
especially iron from the spinach. Eat it as a snack, with salad
as a light meal or take a slice to work as a packed lunch.**

1 Preheat the oven to 190°C/375°F/gas mark 5. Lightly
brush a deep 30 x 20cm/12 x 8in ovenproof dish or
baking pan with olive oil.

2 Put the damp spinach leaves into a large saucepan.
Cover with a lid and cook over a medium heat for
2–3 minutes, shaking the pan a few times, until the
spinach wilts. Drain in a colander, pressing down hard
with a small plate or saucer to extract all the excess
water. Put the strained spinach between 2 large pieces
of kitchen paper (paper towels) and press down lightly.
When cool, chop coarsely.

3 Heat the olive oil in a frying pan (skillet) and cook the
spring onions and garlic for 4–5 minutes, or until tender.
Remove and cool.

4 Put the spinach, spring onions, garlic, dill and cheeses
in a bowl. Stir in the lemon zest, nutmeg and beaten
eggs. Season with pepper – don't add any salt as the
feta is salty.

Continued overleaf →

5 Place a sheet of filo pastry in the oiled dish and brush lightly with olive oil. Add 5 more sheets, brushing in between in the same way, so you end up with 6 layers.

6 Spread the spinach mixture over the pastry and level the top. Cover with a sheet of filo pastry, brushing it lightly with oil, and then add the remaining 5 sheets in the same way.

7 Brush the top of the pie with oil, then bake in the preheated oven for 30–40 minutes until crisp and golden brown. Remove from the oven and stand for a few minutes before cutting into squares or slices. Serve lukewarm or cold.

Tip: While you assemble the pie, make sure you cover the pack of filo pastry with a clean damp cloth to prevent it drying out and cracking.

VARIATIONS
- Use grated Parmesan if you can't find any hard Greek cheese for grating.
- Cook a sliced leek with the spring onions and garlic.

ROLLED VEGAN SPINACH PIE

SERVES 6
PREP: 30 MINUTES
COOK: 1 HOUR

HORTOPITA

1.5kg/3lb spinach and/or a selection of greens, washed and hard stalks removed (see note)

3 tbsp olive oil, plus extra for brushing

2 large leeks, washed, trimmed and thinly sliced

a large bunch of spring onions (scallions), thinly sliced

3 garlic cloves, crushed

a bunch of dill, finely chopped

a bunch of mint, finely chopped

grated zest and juice of 1 lemon

400g/14oz pack filo (phyllo) pastry

sesame seeds, for sprinkling

sea salt and freshly ground black pepper

In this recipe, the spinach filling is rolled up inside the filo (phyllo) pastry and then curled into a spiral shape, like a snail's shell or Cumberland sausage. This dairy-free pie is made during Greek Orthodox Lent, when people fast and abstain from foods that come from blood animals.

1 Put the damp spinach or wild green leaves in a large saucepan set over a high heat. Cover the pan and cook, shaking occasionally, for 3–4 minutes, or until the leaves wilt and soften. Drain in a colander, pressing down well with a small plate or saucer to squeeze out any excess moisture, and then chop coarsely.

2 Heat the olive oil in a large frying pan (skillet) set over a low–medium heat and cook the leeks, stirring occasionally, for 6–8 minutes, or until tender. Stir in the spring onions and garlic and cook for 2–3 minutes, then add the herbs and greens and warm through. Stir in the lemon zest and juice and season to taste with salt and pepper.

3 Preheat the oven to 190°C/375°F/gas mark 5.

4 Unroll the filo pastry and spread out a large sheet on a clean work surface. Only remove the sheets as and when you need them and keep the unused sheets covered with a damp tea (dish) towel while you work, to prevent them drying out. Lightly brush the sheet with olive oil and place another sheet on top. Continue layering the sheets in this way, brushing each one with oil, until they are all used up.

Note: You can mix the spinach with other greens (cultivated and wild), including the following: spring greens, spinach, kale, beet and turnip tops, mustard greens, sorrel, chard, rocket (arugula), dandelion leaves, purslane, amaranth.

5 Place the filling in a long, thick cylindrical shape along one long side of the filo pastry rectangle, leaving a 2.5cm/1in border along the edge. Now roll up the pastry from that long side over the filling and keep rolling like a cigar. You will end up with a stuffed long cylinder.

6 Place the filled pastry cylinder, seam-side down, on the work surface. Working from one end, start coiling it round into a concentric spiral shape like a snail's shell, brushing with oil as you go, so that the coils stick together.

7 Lift it carefully and place in an oiled round ovenproof dish that is large enough to hold it, or on an oiled baking tray. Lightly brush the top with oil and sprinkle with sesame seeds. Bake in the preheated oven for 40 minutes, or until the pastry is crisp and golden brown.

8 Allow to cool a little before cutting the pie into wedges. Serve warm or at room temperature.

VARIATIONS
- Add some chopped fennel herb or flat-leaf (Italian) parsley.
- Add crushed chilli or red chilli flakes.
- Add some grated vegan 'cheese'.

CHICKEN WITH ORZO

SERVES 4
PREP: 10 MINUTES
COOK: 35 MINUTES

GIOUVETSI KOTOPOULO

4 tbsp olive oil
1 large red onion, diced
500g/1lb 2oz skinned,
   boned chicken breasts
   or thighs, cubed
325g/11oz (1½ cups) orzo
   (dry weight)
400g/14oz (2 cups) canned
   chopped tomatoes
2 tbsp tomato paste
1 tsp sugar
720ml/24fl oz (3 cups) hot
   chicken stock or water
juice of 1 lemon
1 tsp ground cinnamon
a pinch of dried oregano
50g/2oz (¼ cup) crumbled
   mizithra or feta cheese
sea salt and freshly ground
   black pepper

This is Greek comfort food – a hearty, rib-sticking dish to warm you up on cold days. Our version is a quick and easy variation on the traditional recipe, which is usually made with beef or lamb and then slow-cooked for several hours in a pot in the oven. Beloved of the Greeks, orzo is a type of pasta shaped like small grains of rice.

1 Heat 2 tablespoons of the olive oil in a large deep frying pan (skillet) set over a medium heat. Add the onion and cook, stirring occasionally, for 6–8 minutes until tender. Stir in the chicken and cook, turning it occasionally, for 5 minutes, or until golden brown all over. Season with salt and pepper and remove from the pan. Set aside while you cook the orzo.

2 Add the remaining oil to the pan together with the orzo and cook for 1–2 minutes, stirring. Add the tomatoes, tomato paste, sugar, half of the chicken stock or water, the lemon juice, cinnamon and oregano, and stir well.

3 Return the chicken and onion to the pan and give everything a good stir. Cover with a lid and cook for 20 minutes. Every 5 minutes or so, uncover and add some more stock as the orzo absorbs it. Stir often and don't let it dry out or stick to the pan.

4 When the orzo is tender but not mushy and the liquid has been absorbed or reduced to a creamy sauce, check the seasoning and remove from the heat.

5 Let it stand for 5 minutes or so before serving sprinkled with crumbled cheese.

VARIATIONS
- Substitute passata for some of the chicken stock.
- Sprinkle with grated Parmesan.
- Add some red wine with the stock.

Tip: We've used boned chicken breasts for speed, try chicken thighs or legs on the bone for more flavour.

BAKED STUFFED VEGETABLES

GEMISTA

4 large beefsteak tomatoes
4 large red or green (bell)
  peppers
olive oil, for drizzling
crusty bread, to serve

FILLING:
a pinch of sugar
6 tbsp olive oil
2 red onions, diced
3 garlic cloves, crushed
1 tbsp crushed fennel seeds
a pinch of ground cinnamon
225g/8oz (1 cup) risotto rice,
  e.g. arborio (dry weight)
150ml/¼ pint (generous
  ½ cup) water
1 tsp tomato paste
a few basil leaves, chopped
a handful of dill, chopped
3 tbsp pine nuts
sea salt and freshly ground
  black pepper

These tasty stuffed vegetables are served in every Greek home and taverna, especially in summer. You can make them up to 2 days in advance and keep them in the fridge. Remove and bring them up to room temperature before serving. The flavours will develop and improve as time goes by.

1 Preheat the oven to 190°C/375°F/gas mark 5.

2 Cut the tops off the tomatoes and peppers and set aside. Hollow out the tomatoes, removing the seeds and pulp to a bowl. Add the sugar to the pulp in a bowl and set aside to use in the filling. Remove the white ribs and seeds from the peppers and discard.

3 To make the rice filling, heat the olive oil in a large frying pan (skillet) set over a medium heat. Cook the onions and garlic, stirring occasionally, for 5 minutes. Stir in the fennel seeds, cinnamon and rice and cook for 2 minutes. Add the water, tomato paste and reserved tomato pulp and cook over a low heat, stirring occasionally, for 5 minutes. Add the herbs and pine nuts and turn off the heat. Season with salt and pepper.

4 Stuff the tomatoes and peppers with the rice filling, leaving a little space at the top for the rice to plump up and expand while cooking. Cover with the reserved 'lids', and place in an ovenproof baking dish, packing them in tightly so they don't fall over. Drizzle generously with olive oil and pour a little water into the baking dish around the vegetables.

Continued overleaf →

5 Bake in the preheated oven for 1–1¼ hours or until the vegetables are cooked but still hold their shape and the rice is tender. Turn off the oven and leave them for 10 minutes before removing.

6 Serve warm or at room temperature with crusty bread to mop up the olive oil and juices.

Tip: Check the vegetables while they are cooking. If they are browning on top, cover with some kitchen foil (aluminum foil).

VARIATIONS
- Substitute aubergines (eggplants) and courgettes (zucchini) for the tomatoes and peppers. Add the scooped-out flesh to the rice filling.
- Add some currants or chopped walnuts to the filling.
- Serve with salty feta cheese.

VEGAN MOUSSAKA

SERVES 4
PREP: 20 MINUTES
COOK: 1¼ HOURS

4 aubergines (eggplants), trimmed

2 tbsp olive oil, plus extra for brushing

150g/5oz (generous 2 cups) organic vegan soya mince (dry weight)

1 large red onion, finely chopped

3 garlic cloves, crushed

450g/1lb mushrooms, diced

400g/14oz (2 cups) canned chopped tomatoes

1 tbsp tomato paste

a good pinch of sugar

a few sprigs of basil, chopped

a small handful of flat-leaf (Italian) parsley, chopped

2 tbsp grated vegan Parmesan cheese

Here's a delicious moussaka with a vegan soya mince and mushroom filling. You can use any fresh mushrooms or a mixture of fresh and dried. If you've never used soya mince before, you'll be pleasantly surprised at how easy it is to cook with and how good it tastes. In this recipe, we bake rather than fry the sliced aubergine (eggplant) to make it less oily.

1 Preheat the oven to 180°C/350°F/gas mark 4. Lightly oil 2 baking trays.

2 Thinly slice 3 aubergines and place in a single layer on the oiled baking trays. Brush lightly with olive oil and season with salt and pepper. Bake in the preheated oven for 15–20 minutes, or until tender and golden brown.

3 Put the soya mince in a bowl and soak in boiling or hot water, following the instructions on the packet. Drain well and squeeze out any excess water.

4 Meanwhile, heat the 2 tablespoons of olive oil in a large frying pan (skillet) set over a low heat. Cook the onion and garlic, stirring occasionally, for 10 minutes, or until softened.

5 Dice the remaining aubergine and add to the pan with the mushrooms and cook, stirring, for 5 minutes, or until tender and golden. Add the tomatoes and tomato paste and cook for 5 minutes, then stir in the drained soya mince. Continue cooking until the sauce reduces and thickens (about 5 minutes). Stir in the sugar, basil and parsley and season to taste with salt and pepper.

BÉCHAMEL SAUCE:
50g/2oz (¼ cup) vegan
    butter
50g/2oz (½ cup) plain
    (all-purpose) flour
480ml/16fl oz (2 cups)
    dairy-free oat or nut milk
50g/2oz (½ cup) grated
    vegan Parmesan cheese
    (e.g. Violife)
a pinch of freshly grated
    nutmeg
sea salt and freshly ground
    black pepper

6 To make the béchamel sauce, melt the butter in a saucepan set over a low heat and stir in the flour with a wooden spoon. Cook for 1–2 minutes until it starts to colour and smell nutty, then beat in the milk, a little at a time, until smooth and free from lumps. Turn up the heat and stir until the sauce is thick and smooth. Remove from the heat and beat in the cheese and nutmeg. Season to taste.

7 Arrange half of the baked aubergine slices in the bottom of a large ovenproof dish. Pour in the soya mince and mushroom mixture, then cover with the remaining aubergine slices. Pour the béchamel sauce over the top and sprinkle with grated cheese.

8 Bake in the preheated oven for 35–40 minutes, or until golden brown. Allow to cool for 5–10 minutes before cutting into squares.

Tip: If using dried porcini, soak in a little warm water and add with the soaking water to the moussaka sauce or substitute the soaking water for some of the milk in the béchamel.

VARIATIONS
• Fry the aubergine (eggplant) slices in oil instead of baking them. Or cook on an oiled hot griddle (grill) pan.
• Add a little red wine to the sauce.

GREEN ORZO 'RISOTTO'

SERVES 4
PREP: 10 MINUTES
COOK: 35 MINUTES

200g/7oz spinach, washed
and trimmed
3 tbsp butter
4 tbsp olive oil
1 large onion, chopped
2 garlic cloves, crushed
300g/10oz thin asparagus,
trimmed and cut into
2.5cm/1in lengths
350g/12oz (1½ cups) orzo
(dry weight)
1.1 litres/40fl oz (5 cups)
hot vegetable stock
75g/3oz (½ cup) frozen peas
grated zest and juice of
1 lemon
50g/2oz (½ cup) grated
Kefalotyri or Parmesan
cheese, plus extra for
sprinkling
sea salt and freshly ground
black pepper

This creamy green 'risotto' is coloured with spinach and uses rice-shaped orzo pasta. It's easier to make than a classic rice risotto because you don't have to add the stock gradually and stir it constantly as it cooks.

1 Put the spinach in a colander and pour over 2 kettles of boiling water until it wilts. Press down on it with a small plate or saucer to squeeze out the excess liquid. Transfer to a food processor or food chopper and blitz with 2 tablespoons of butter to a smooth purée. Set aside.

2 Heat the olive oil in a large frying pan (skillet) set over a medium heat. Cook the onion and garlic, stirring occasionally, for 6–8 minutes, or until tender. Add the asparagus stems (not the tips) and cook gently for 2 minutes.

3 Stir in the orzo and cook for 2–3 minutes. Add most of the hot stock and bring to the boil. Reduce the heat to low and simmer gently, stirring occasionally, for 20 minutes, or until the orzo is tender and al dente and the liquid has been absorbed. If the orzo soaks up all the liquid before it is tender, just add the remaining stock. Stir in the asparagus tips and peas 5 minutes before the end of the cooking time.

4 Take the pan off the heat and gently stir in the spinach purée, lemon zest and juice, grated cheese and remaining tablespoon of butter. Season to taste with salt and pepper.

5 Divide the risotto between 4 shallow serving bowls and serve immediately, sprinkled with grated cheese.

VARIATIONS
• Add sliced courgettes (zucchini) or fine green beans.
• Stir in some chopped dill, mint or parsley.

BEEF STEW

STIFADO

SERVES 4
PREP: 15 MINUTES
COOK: 2–2½ HOURS

4 tbsp olive oil
1kg/2¼lb stewing beef,
   e.g. chuck steak or skirt,
   cubed
600g/1lb 5oz small pickling
   (pearl) onions or shallots,
   peeled
a good pinch of sugar
3 garlic cloves, crushed
a pinch of ground allspice
a pinch of ground nutmeg
1 tbsp tomato paste
240ml/8fl oz (1 cup) red
   wine
2 tbsp red wine vinegar
400g/14oz (2 cups) canned
   chopped tomatoes
1 beef stock (bouillon) cube
   or stock 'pot'
a pinch of dried oregano
2 bay leaves
1 cinnamon stick
sea salt and freshly ground
   black pepper
orzo, rice or mashed or
   boiled potatoes, to serve

Always use a good cut of stewing beef to make this rustic stew. The cooked meat should be melt-in-the-mouth fork-tender. For the best flavour, make the *stifado* a day ahead and reheat it the following day when the flavours have intensified. It can also be cooled and then frozen for up to 3 months.

1 Heat the oil in a large saucepan set over a medium–high heat. Add the beef and cook, stirring and turning often, for 6–8 minutes, or until it is seared and browned all over. Remove from the pan and set aside.

2 Reduce the heat to medium and add the onions to the pan. Cook, stirring occasionally, for 8–10 minutes, or until they are golden brown all over. Stir in the sugar and cook for 1–2 minutes.

3 Stir in the garlic, ground spices and tomato paste and cook for 1 minute. Add the wine, vinegar and tomatoes. Fill the drained tomato can with water and add to the pan, then repeat. Add the stock cube, oregano, bay leaves and cinnamon stick.

4 Return the beef to the pan and stir well, then bring to the boil. Reduce the heat to low and simmer gently for 1½–2 hours, or until the beef is really tender and the liquid has reduced to an aromatic sauce. Be sure to check on it every 15–20 minutes, adding more water if needed. Do not let it dry out or catch on the bottom of the pan.

5 Season to taste with salt and pepper and serve hot with orzo, rice or mashed or boiled potatoes.

VARIATIONS
- Add some freshly stripped thyme or rosemary leaves.
- Serve sprinkled with chopped flat-leaf (Italian) parsley.
- Enhance the flavour by adding a little brandy.

KOKKINISTO

This beef stew, flavoured with cinnamon and cloves, is an everyday, simpler version of *stifado*. It's usually served with bucatini, a spaghetti-type pasta with a hole in the centre, but you could use any tubular pasta or thick spaghetti.

1 As above, brown the beef in oil over a high heat and remove from the pan. Fry a large chopped red onion with the garlic and stir in some ground cloves and cinnamon (or use 2 whole cloves and a cinnamon stick). Continue as above, with the tomato paste, red wine, sugar and 4 chopped fresh tomatoes (not canned).

2 Bring to the boil, then return the beef to the pan and cover with hot water. Reduce the heat to low and simmer, covered with a lid, for 2–2½ hours, or until the liquid reduces and the beef is really tender. Or transfer to a casserole dish and cook in a low oven.

3 Serve drizzled with olive oil and sprinkled with grated Kefalotyri cheese, with some tubular pasta.

BEEF & AUBERGINE BAKE

SERVES 6
PREP: 20 MINUTES
SALT: 30 MINUTES
COOK: 1–1¼ HOURS

MOUSSAKA

3 aubergines (eggplants),
    cut into 1cm/½in-thick
    slices
2 tbsp olive oil, plus extra
    for frying and brushing
1 large onion, chopped
1 garlic clove, crushed
450g/1lb (2 cups) minced
    (ground) lean beef
1 tbsp tomato paste
400g/14oz (2 cups) canned
    tomatoes
1 tsp sugar
120ml/4fl oz (½ cup) red
    wine
1 cinnamon stick
1 bay leaf
a pinch of dried oregano
sea salt and freshly ground
    black pepper

This appetizing layered dish used to be made in huge trays in Greek villages to serve whole families and crowds of people. Everything could be assembled in advance and cooked later in the day or even reheated the following day. It's comfort food at its best.

1 Put the aubergines in a colander and sprinkle them with salt. Leave them for at least 30 minutes to exude their bitter juice, then rinse well and pat dry with kitchen paper (paper towels).

2 Heat plenty of oil in a large frying pan (skillet) set over a medium–high heat, and fry the aubergine slices, in batches, until golden brown on both sides. Remove from the pan and drain on kitchen paper.

3 To make the meat sauce, heat the 2 tablespoons of olive oil in a pan set over a medium–high heat. Add the onion and garlic and cook for 4–5 minutes, or until softened. Add the minced beef and cook, stirring, until browned all over. Stir in the tomato paste, tomatoes, sugar and red wine together with the cinnamon and herbs.

4 Season with salt and pepper and bring to the boil. Turn down the heat to low and cook gently for 15 minutes, stirring occasionally, until the liquid reduces and thickens. Discard the bay leaf and cinnamon stick.

5 Meanwhile, make the béchamel sauce. Melt the butter in a saucepan over a low heat and stir in the flour with a wooden spoon. Cook for 1–2 minutes until it starts to colour and smell nutty, then beat in the milk, a little at a time, until smooth and free from lumps.

82

BÉCHAMEL SAUCE:
50g/2oz (¼ cup) butter
50g/2oz (½ cup) plain
(all-purpose) flour
480ml/16fl oz (2 cups) milk
2 medium free-range egg
yolks, beaten
a pinch of freshly grated
nutmeg
75g/3oz (¾ cup) grated
Kefalotyri or Parmesan
cheese

Turn up the heat and stir until the sauce is thick and smooth. Off the heat, beat in the egg yolks and nutmeg, and then most of the cheese, reserving some for the topping. Season to taste with salt and pepper.

6 Preheat the oven to 180°C/350°F/gas mark 4. Lightly oil or butter a large, deep baking dish.

7 To assemble the moussaka, arrange half of the fried aubergine slices in the base of the dish. Mix 2 tablespoons of the béchamel sauce into the meat sauce and pour over the aubergines. Smooth the top, then cover with the remaining fried aubergines. Spread the rest of the béchamel sauce over the top and sprinkle with the remaining grated cheese.

8 Cook in the preheated oven for 30–40 minutes, or until the top is set and golden brown. Set aside to cool for 10 minutes before cutting into squares.

VARIATIONS
- Lightly oil the aubergine (eggplant) slices and bake in the oven instead of frying them.
- Use sliced potatoes instead of the aubergine or a mixture of potatoes and aubergine.
- Add some chopped parsley or basil to the meat sauce.
- Add a dash of red wine vinegar to the meat sauce.

GREEK BAKED FISH

PSARI PLAKI

SERVES 4
PREP: 10 MINUTES
MARINATE: 30 MINUTES
COOK: 40–50 MINUTES

1kg/2¼lb firm white fish fillets, e.g. cod, cut into large pieces
juice of 1 lemon
3 tbsp olive oil
3 onions, thinly sliced
3 garlic cloves, crushed
900g/2lb ripe tomatoes, chopped
1 tbsp tomato paste
a pinch of sugar
1 tsp dried oregano
120ml/4fl oz (½ cup) red wine
12 black Kalamata olives, stoned (pitted)
a handful of flat-leaf (Italian) parsley, chopped
sea salt and freshly ground black pepper
boiled potatoes, to serve

This is such a wonderful, easy recipe to prepare and cook. Serve it lukewarm in the summer with a warm potato salad (see page 109) or piping hot in the winter with boiled potatoes or rice. It's nutritious, healthy, colourful ... what's not to like?

1 Put the fish in a large baking dish and pour over the lemon juice. Season with salt and pepper. Cover and leave in a cool place to marinate for 30 minutes.

2 Preheat the oven to 180°C/350°F/gas mark 4.

3 Heat the oil in a large frying pan (skillet) set over a low–medium heat. Cook the onions and garlic, stirring occasionally, for 10 minutes, or until tender. Add the tomatoes, tomato paste, sugar, oregano and wine. Cook, uncovered, for 10–15 minutes until the sauce thickens and reduces. Stir in the olives and most of the parsley, reserving some for the garnish.

4 Pour the sauce over the fish and bake in the preheated oven for 20–25 minutes, or until the fish is cooked and opaque. Sprinkle with the remaining parsley and serve with boiled potatoes.

Tip: If fresh tomatoes are not in season, use 2 x 400g/14oz cans of chopped tomatoes instead.

VARIATIONS
• Add some capers to the tomato sauce.
• Add ½ teaspoon of clear honey to the sauce, if wished.
• Stir in some chopped basil.

GREEK 'LASAGNE'

PASTITSIO

SERVES 4
PREP: 20 MINUTES
COOK: 1¼–1½ HOURS

2 tbsp olive oil
1 large red onion, diced
2 garlic cloves, crushed
450g/1lb (2 cups) minced
   (ground) lean beef
120ml/4fl oz (½ cup) red
   wine
1 tbsp tomato paste
400g/14oz (2 cups) canned
   chopped tomatoes
a good pinch of sugar
1 bay leaf
½ tsp ground cinnamon
a small handful of flat-leaf
   (Italian) parsley, chopped
200g/7oz ziti or bucatini
   pasta (dry weight)
sea salt and freshly ground
   black pepper

BÉCHAMEL SAUCE:
50g/2oz (¼ cup) butter
50g/2oz (½ cup) plain
   (all-purpose) flour
480ml/16fl oz (2 cups) milk
2 medium free-range egg
   yolks, beaten
a pinch of freshly grated
   nutmeg
75g/3oz (¾ cup) grated
   Kefalotyri or Parmesan
   cheese

This layered dish of small pasta tubes covered with a tasty meat sauce and topped with a creamy béchamel is often called Greek 'lasagne'. It's much simpler to make than it looks and is perfect for cold winter days. In Greece, it is eaten all the year round – with a crisp salad or _horiatiki_ (see page 94) in summer.

1 To make the meat sauce, heat the olive oil in a saucepan set over a medium heat and cook the onion and garlic, stirring occasionally, for 5 minutes or until they start to soften.

2 Stir in the minced beef and cook, stirring occasionally, for 5 minutes, or until browned all over. Add the red wine and cook for 3–4 minutes until it evaporates. Stir in the tomato paste, tomatoes, sugar, bay leaf and cinnamon, and turn up the heat. As soon as it boils, reduce the heat and cover the pan. Simmer gently for 20–25 minutes, or until the sauce reduces and thickens – it should not be runny. Stir in the parsley and discard the bay leaf, then season to taste with salt and pepper.

3 Meanwhile, make the béchamel sauce: melt the butter in a saucepan over a low heat and stir in the flour with a wooden spoon. Cook for 1–2 minutes until it starts to colour and smell nutty, then beat in the milk, a little at a time, until smooth and free from lumps. Turn up the heat and stir until the sauce is thick and smooth. Off the heat, beat in the eggs and nutmeg, and then most of the cheese, reserving some for the topping. Season to taste with salt and pepper.

4 Preheat the oven to 180°C/350°F/gas mark 4. Oil or butter a large deep baking dish.

VARIATIONS
- For a more highly flavoured meat sauce, add a beef stock cube or bouillon powder.
- Crumble some feta cheese over the pasta layer before adding the meat sauce.

5 Cook the pasta according to the packet instructions and drain well. Do not overcook – you want it to be firm and *al dente* and to retain a little 'bite'.

6 Transfer the cooked pasta to the baking dish in a single layer. Cover with the meat sauce, levelling the top. Spoon the béchamel over the top and sprinkle with the remaining grated cheese.

7 Bake in the preheated oven for 30–40 minutes, or until the top is set and golden brown. Set aside to cool for 10 minutes before cutting into squares.

MEATBALL SOUP

YOUVARLAKIA

SERVES 4
PREP: 20 MINUTES
CHILL: 15–30 MINUTES
COOK: 30 MINUTES

500g/1lb 2oz (2¼ cups) lean
   minced (ground) beef
50g/2oz (¼ cup) risotto rice,
   e.g. arborio (dry weight)
1 onion, diced
1 garlic clove, crushed
a handful of flat-leaf
   (Italian) parsley, finely
   chopped
2 tbsp olive oil
1 medium free-range egg,
   beaten
900ml/1½ pints (3¾ cups)
   chicken or vegetable stock
sea salt and freshly ground
   black pepper
chopped dill, for sprinkling
crusty bread, to serve

AVGOLEMONO:
3 medium free-range eggs
   (at room temperature)
juice of 2 lemons

VARIATIONS
- Add some chopped
  dill to the meatball
  mixture.
- Whisk some grated
  lemon zest with the
  lemon juice and eggs.

With its clean, fresh, lemony flavour, *avgolemono* is the most popular sauce in Greece. Here, it is thinned down to make a wonderfully aromatic and fragrant soup, which is traditionally served in winter.

1 To make the meatballs, put the minced beef, rice, onion, garlic, parsley, olive oil and beaten egg in a bowl and mix together until well combined. Cover with some clingfilm (plastic wrap) and chill in the fridge for 15–30 minutes. Don't be tempted to skip this step – it helps to keep the meatballs firm.

2 Using your hands, take small amounts of the mixture and mould into small balls, about 20 in total.

3 Pour the stock into a wide saucepan and bring to the boil. Reduce the heat to low and carefully add the meatballs. Cover the pan and cook gently for 20–25 minutes, checking occasionally to make sure that there is plenty of liquid.

4 Turn off the heat and remove the meatballs with a slotted spoon. Keep warm. Set aside the pan of hot stock for 10 minutes to cool it down.

5 To make the *avgolemono*, beat the eggs in a large bowl, using a hand-held electric whisk. Add the lemon juice and whisk well. Slowly pour a ladle of the stock on to the egg and lemon mixture, whisking all the time, and then whisk in another ladleful until smooth.

6 Add to the remaining hot stock in the pan and stir gently. Set over a low–medium heat and stir for 4–5 minutes until thickened and warmed through. Do *not* allow it to boil.

7 Return the meatballs to the pan and simmer gently for a few minutes and then serve, sprinkled with dill, with crusty bread on the side.

GREEK ROAST LAMB

KLEFTIKO

SERVES 6
PREP: 25 MINUTES
MARINATE:
OVERNIGHT
COOK: 4½–5 HOURS

1.5kg/3lb leg of lamb on
  the bone
1kg/2¼lb potatoes, peeled
  and quartered
3 tbsp olive oil
juice of 1 lemon
2 red onions, cut into wedges
sea salt and freshly ground
  black pepper

This method of slow-cooking lamb and potatoes in a lemony, garlic marinade is so delicious. The meat is meltingly tender, and the crispy potatoes are suffused with lemon juice. We have used large fluffy potatoes, such as Desirée, but you could substitute Charlotte or new potatoes and use them whole or halved.

1 To make the marinade, crush the garlic cloves with the salt using a pestle and mortar. Add a grinding of black pepper, the cinnamon, lemon zest and herbs, crushing everything together. Stir in the olive oil and lemon juice. Or blitz everything in a blender.

2 Rub the marinade all over the leg of lamb, making a few slits with a sharp knife so the aromatic paste can penetrate the meat. Place in a bowl, cover and leave in the fridge or a cool place overnight.

3 The following day, preheat the oven to 170°C/325°F/gas mark 3. Take a large sheet of baking parchment and place it on top of a large sheet of kitchen foil (aluminum foil).

4 Toss the potatoes in the olive oil and lemon juice and arrange in the middle of the baking parchment with the onion wedges. Season with salt and pepper. Place the marinated lamb on top and lift the sides of the parchment and foil over the potatoes and lamb so the edges meet above them in the middle. Scrunch them together to seal the parcel. If wished, secure with some kitchen string.

5 Transfer to a large roasting pan and bake in the oven for 3½ hours. Increase the oven temperature to 200°C/400°F/gas mark 6 and remove the roasting pan. Open the parcel and fold back the sides, then return to the oven for 30–40 minutes, or until the lamb is browned.

VARIATIONS
- Add a pinch of crushed chilli flakes to the marinade.
- Add some chunks of red and green (bell) peppers with the potatoes.
- Use 6 individual lamb shanks instead of a large leg of lamb. Or ask the butcher to cut the leg of lamb into 6 pieces on the bone.

MARINADE:

4 garlic cloves, peeled
1 tsp sea salt
freshly ground black pepper
½ tsp ground cinnamon
grated zest and juice of
    1 lemon
5 oregano sprigs, leaves
    picked
2 rosemary sprigs, leaves
    picked
3 tbsp olive oil

6 Remove the lamb, cover with a fresh sheet of foil and set aside to rest on a board for 15–20 minutes before carving.

7 Meanwhile, pop the pan back into the oven for 15 minutes, or until the potatoes crisp up. Serve immediately with the red onions and lamb.

> **Tip: Cubes of hard cheese (Graviera or Kefalotyri) are sometimes added to the pan before cooking, or feta may be crumbled over the top before serving.**

SALADS & SIDES

ΣΑΛΑΤΕΣ & ΟΣΠΡΙΑ

GREEK VILLAGE SALAD

SERVES 4
PREP: 10 MINUTES

HORIATIKI

4 large ripe tomatoes, cut
   into wedges
1 yellow (bell) pepper,
   deseeded and sliced
1 small (Lebanese)
   cucumber, peeled
   (optional) and sliced
½ small red onion, thinly
   sliced
16 black olives
a good pinch of sea salt
½ tsp dried oregano
200g/7oz feta, diced
fruity olive oil, for drizzling
a dash of red wine vinegar

This is the classic humble village salad that is eaten in every home, taverna, beach bar and restaurant all over Greece. Traditionally, the salad is not tossed in a dressing. Instead, the oil and vinegar are drizzled over the top before serving, or people add it themselves. For the most delicious and most authentic result, use the best-quality ingredients you can source – sweet and fragrant locally grown tomatoes, juicy black olives and fruity green extra virgin olive oil.

1 Put the tomatoes, yellow pepper, cucumber and red onion in a bowl. Add the olives and stir well.

2 Sprinkle with sea salt and oregano and scatter the feta over the top.

3 Drizzle with olive oil and a dash of vinegar.

Tip: If you can't get hold of a small Greek or ridged cucumber, use ½ English cucumber, cut into chunks or thickish slices.

VARIATIONS
• Add some capers or chopped fresh flat-leaf (Italian) parsley, mint or Greek basil.
• Instead of vinegar, add squeeze of lemon juice.
• Rather than dice or crumble the feta, just place a thick slice on top for people to help themselves.

94

BARLEY RUSK & TOMATO SALAD

SERVES 4
PREP: 10 MINUTES

KRITIKOS DAKOS

4 Greek dry barley rusks
fruity olive oil, for drizzling
4 large ripe vine tomatoes
200g/7oz feta
1 tsp dried oregano
8 Kalamata olives
½ small red onion, thinly
 sliced
sea salt

Note: You can buy Greek barley rusks online or from specialist suppliers and delicatessens.

Tip: Don't soak the rusks for too long or they will be too soggy. You want them to retain a little crunch. You can pass them quickly under a running cold tap instead of soaking them, if wished.

This simple Cretan salad is made with soaked barley rusks and fragrant tomatoes. It's the perfect dish for a hot summer's day – the Greek equivalent of the Tuscan *panzanella* salad, which is made with stale bread. Serve it as part of a *meze* spread with some fried or griddled halloumi, some *dolmades* (see page 14) and a selection of dips.

1 Put the rusks in a bowl and cover with cold water. Leave to soak for 1 minute, then remove the rusks and place on a large serving plate. Drizzle generously with olive oil and season with salt.

2 Coarsely grate 2 tomatoes over a bowl to make a liquid tomato sauce. Finely slice the remaining tomatoes. Lightly season both with salt to bring out the flavour and aroma.

3 Spoon the liquid tomato sauce over the top of the rusks, so they soak it up. Cover with the sliced tomatoes and crumble the feta over the top.

4 Sprinkle with the oregano and garnish with the olives and red onion. Drizzle generously with olive oil and serve immediately.

VARIATIONS
• Instead of feta, use mizithra cheese or even some creamy soft cheese.
• Add some capers and fresh basil.
• Add a dash of red wine vinegar.

96

GREEK WILD GREENS

HORTA

1.5kg/3lb mixed greens
   (see below)
4 tbsp olive oil
juice of 1 large lemon
a handful of dill, chopped
sea salt
lemon wedges and olive
   oil, to serve

Collard greens: spring
   greens, spinach, kale,
   beet and turnip tops,
   mustard greens

Wild greens: sorrel,
   chard, rocket (arugula),
   dandelion leaves,
   purslane, amaranth

Green leafy vegetables are among the healthiest foods you can eat, and *horta*, the Greek way of cooking and serving them, is so delicious. It's important to use the freshest greens you can find. In Greece, that means gathering them yourself in the wild. However, if you can't do this, just buy the best-quality ones available in your local food store or farmers' market.

1 Wash the greens thoroughly under running cold water, especially if they have been picked in the wild. Pat dry with kitchen paper (paper towels) and discard any tough woody stems and stalks.

2 Cook in a steamer or a colander suspended over a pan of simmering water for 2–3 minutes, or until the leaves wilt and are just tender. Drain and plunge them into a bowl of iced water to stop them cooking and keep them green. Drain, pat dry and transfer to a bowl.

3 Whisk together the olive oil and lemon juice and use to gently toss the greens and dill. Season to taste with salt.

4 Transfer to a serving bowl or plate and serve at room temperature with lemon wedges for squeezing and more olive oil for drizzling.

> **Tip: If you want to eat this as a hot vegetable dish, don't immerse the steamed greens in iced water. Instead, dress them with the oil and lemon, season to taste and serve lukewarm.**

OREGANO POTATO FRIES WITH FETA

SERVES 4
PREP: 10 MINUTES
COOK: 10–12 MINUTES

6 potatoes, peeled
1 tsp sea salt
olive oil, for frying
2 tsp dried oregano
200g/7oz feta, crumbled

There's a lot of discussion about double-, triple- and even quadruple-cooked fries but the best ones of all are Greek oregano fries, sprinkled with salty feta. They're as good as it gets!

1 Slice the potatoes into 1cm/½in-thick slices and then cut each of these into 1cm/½in-wide finger-size chips (fries). Sprinkle lightly with salt.

2 Heat the oil in a deep-fat fryer or a large deep saucepan. When it reaches 180°C/350°F (use a sugar thermometer to check this), add the potatoes, a few at a time, and fry in batches for 3–4 minutes or until golden brown and crisp on the outside and fluffy on the inside.

3 Remove with a slotted spoon and drain on kitchen paper (paper towels).

4 Sprinkle with salt and oregano, then serve immediately with the crumbled feta scattered over the top.

Tip: Note that it's very important to use potato varieties that are good for frying, such as Maris Piper, Russet or Kennebec.

GREEK ROASTED VEGETABLES

BRIAM

SERVES 4–6
PREP: 15 MINUTES
COOK: 1–1½ HOURS

1 large aubergine (eggplant), trimmed and cut into 1cm/½in slices

2 courgettes (zucchini), trimmed and cut into 1cm/½in slices

1 red (bell) pepper, deseeded and cut into chunks

1 green (bell) pepper, deseeded and cut into chunks

3 potatoes, peeled and thickly sliced or cut into chunks

2 red onions, sliced

450g/1lb ripe tomatoes, sliced

2 garlic cloves, crushed

6 tbsp olive oil, plus extra for drizzling

a few sprigs oregano and thyme, leaves picked

sea salt and freshly ground black pepper

TO SERVE:
crumbled feta cheese (optional)
chopped flat-leaf (Italian) parsley (optional)
crusty bread

Many years ago, this traditional dish was prepared at home in large trays and then taken to the village bakery to be cooked in the communal bread oven. Simple, delicious and perfect for feeding a crowd with some crusty bread and cheese, *briam* is good to serve at any time of the year.

1 Preheat the oven to 190°C/375°F/gas mark 5.

2 Put all the vegetables in a large ovenproof dish. Sprinkle with the garlic and season with salt and pepper. Pour the olive oil over the top and sprinkle with the oregano and thyme leaves. Add 3–4 tablespoons of water to one corner of the dish to keep the vegetables moist.

3 Bake in the preheated oven for 1–1½ hours, stirring the vegetables every 15 minutes or so and keeping the potatoes near the top so they crisp up nicely. When the vegetables are tender and mellow and the potatoes are golden brown, remove from the oven and cool.

4 Serve at room temperature, drizzled with olive oil. If wished, sprinkle with some crumbled feta and chopped parsley. Eat with crusty bread to mop up all the delicious oil.

VARIATIONS
- Chop or grate the tomatoes instead of slicing them for a moister sauce-type consistency.
- Add a yellow or orange (bell) pepper.
- To make this more substantial, add some green beans.

BAKED BEANS IN TOMATO SAUCE

SERVES 4
SOAK: OVERNIGHT
PREP: 10 MINUTES
COOK: 2½–3 HOURS

GIGANTES PLAKI

300g/10oz (2 cups) dried *gigantes* or butterbeans (lima beans) (dry weight)
6 tbsp fruity olive oil, plus extra for drizzling
1 onion, finely chopped
2 celery sticks, finely chopped
3 garlic cloves, crushed
2 tbsp tomato paste
675g/1½lb ripe plum tomatoes, skinned and roughly chopped
a few oregano sprigs, leaves picked
1 tsp sugar
1 tbsp red wine vinegar
a handful of flat-leaf (Italian) parsley, chopped
115g/4oz feta, crumbled
sea salt and freshly ground black pepper
crusty bread, to serve

You must use dried beans in this recipe and soak them overnight or for up to 24 hours before cooking. Greek *gigantes* beans are available online and in some wholefood stores and delis, but butterbeans work well, too.

1 Put the beans in a large bowl, cover with cold water and leave to soak overnight.

2 The following day, drain the beans and rinse in a colander under cold running water. Transfer to a large saucepan and cover them generously with cold water. Bring to the boil, then reduce the heat to low and simmer for 1 hour, or until the beans are slightly tender but still retain some bite. Take care not to overcook them – they must not be soft. Drain in a colander, reserving the cooking liquid.

3 Preheat the oven to 170°C/325°F/gas mark 3.

4 Heat the olive oil in a pan set over a medium heat. Cook the onion, celery and garlic, stirring occasionally, for 6–8 minutes, or until tender. Stir in the tomato paste and cook for 1 minute. Add the tomatoes, oregano, sugar, vinegar, drained beans and 400ml/14fl oz (1¾ cups) of the reserved cooking liquid. Stir well and season to taste with salt and pepper.

Continued overleaf →

5 Transfer to an ovenproof baking dish or roasting pan and cover with kitchen foil (aluminum foil). Bake in the preheated oven for 1–1¼ hours, then remove the foil and cook for 15–20 minutes, or until the tomato sauce has thickened and the beans are tender.

6 Leave to cool to room temperature. Serve lukewarm, sprinkled with parsley and feta and drizzled with olive oil, with some crusty bread for soaking up the tomato sauce.

VARIATIONS
- Use canned tomatoes instead of fresh ones.
- Add some sliced carrots with the onions, celery and garlic.
- Sprinkle with dill instead of parsley.

Tip: If the liquid evaporates and the beans seem dry when you remove the foil, add some water.

GREEK WHITE BEAN SALAD

FASOLIA

250g/9oz (1¼ cups) small white beans, e.g. haricot or cannellini (dry weight)
2 garlic cloves, crushed
1 bay leaf
2 sprigs of thyme
4 tbsp extra virgin olive oil, plus extra for drizzling
juice of 1 lemon
1 tbsp red wine vinegar
2 large juicy tomatoes, diced
½ small red onion, diced
a handful of flat-leaf (Italian) parsley, chopped
sea salt and freshly ground black pepper

This simple bean salad is a Greek staple. It's very nutritious and packed with protein and dietary fibre. We make it in the traditional way and soak the beans before cooking them from scratch, but if you're in a hurry you could cheat and use canned beans instead. For the best flavour, always use a fruity green olive oil.

1 Put the beans in a bowl, cover with cold water and leave them to soak overnight.

2 The following day, drain the beans in a colander and refresh under cold running water. Transfer them to a large saucepan with the garlic, bay leaf, thyme and olive oil. Pour in enough cold water to cover the beans by at least 2.5cm/1in and bring to the boil.

3 Reduce the heat to a bare simmer and cook gently for about 1½ hours, or until the beans are tender but not mushy. Check them from time to time and add more water if they are getting too dry. Strain and discard the herbs.

4 Put the warm beans in a serving bowl and drizzle with olive oil, the lemon juice and vinegar. Toss lightly together. Stir in the tomatoes and red onion and season to taste with salt and pepper. Leave to cool and serve, lukewarm or cold, sprinkled with parsley.

VARIATIONS
- Use dill or mint instead of parsley.
- Stir in some black olives before serving.
- Crumble some feta over the top of the salad.

LENTIL SALAD

FAKES SALATA

SERVE 4
PREP: 10 MINUTES
COOK: 20–25
MINUTES

250g/9oz (1¼ cups) brown
  lentils (dry weight)
3 tbsp olive oil, plus extra
  for drizzling
1 red onion, chopped
2 garlic cloves, chopped
20 baby plum or cherry
  tomatoes
juice of 1 lemon
a dash of balsamic or red
  wine vinegar
a handful of flat-leaf
  (Italian) parsley, chopped
a few sprigs of basil, leaves
  torn
150g/5oz feta, crumbled
sea salt and freshly ground
  black pepper

**Lentil salads are popular in Greece all the year round and
are often served with grilled (broiled) chicken or fish. Small
brown lentils are usually used but you could make this with
green or Puy lentils instead. However, don't use the small
red ones as they do not keep their shape and cook down to
a soft mush.**

1 Put the lentils in a sieve and rinse under cold running
water. Remove any pieces of grit and tip them into a
saucepan. Cover with cold water and set over a high heat.
When the water boils, reduce the heat to low–medium
and simmer gently for 15–20 minutes, or until the lentils
are just tender but not mushy. Drain well.

2 Meanwhile, heat the olive oil in a large frying pan (skillet)
set over a medium heat and cook the onion and garlic,
stirring occasionally, for 6–8 minutes until softened. Stir
in the tomatoes and cook for 5 minutes until softened,
squashing them with a wooden spoon until they burst.

3 Stir in the drained lentils and mix well. Cook for 5 minutes,
adding a little water to make the mixture moist and creamy.
Add the lemon juice, vinegar and most of the herbs, and
season to taste with salt and pepper.

4 Transfer to a serving dish and drizzle with olive oil.
Sprinkle with the feta and the remaining herbs and serve
lukewarm or at room temperature.

VARIATIONS
- Stir in some juicy
  black olives.
- Add some chopped
  mint.
- Cook the lentils in
  vegetable stock
  instead of water.
- Top with griddled
  sliced halloumi or
  grated cheese
  instead of feta.

BULGUR WHEAT SALAD

SERVES 4
PREP: 15 MINUTES
SOAK: 15 MINUTES

PLIGOURI SALATA

120g/4oz (generous ½ cup) bulgur wheat (dry weight)
240ml/8fl oz (1 cup) boiling water
350g/12oz baby plum or cherry tomatoes, halved
¼ cucumber, cut into chunks
4 spring onions (scallions), thinly sliced
16 black olives, stoned (pitted)
2 tbsp capers, rinsed
a handful of mint, chopped
a handful of flat-leaf (Italian) parsley, chopped
4 tbsp fruity olive oil
juice of 1 large lemon
150g/5oz feta
sea salt and freshly ground black pepper

Bulgur wheat is widely eaten in Greece, usually in *tabbouleh* but also in salads such as this one. We have combined the nutty-tasting grains with traditional village salad (*horiatiki*) ingredients to create a healthy and nutritious light meal.

1 Put the bulgur wheat in a large bowl and pour the boiling water over it. Stir well and cover the bowl with clingfilm (plastic wrap). Leave for 15 minutes, or until the bulgur wheat is tender but still retains some 'bite'. If any excess water remains, drain in a sieve.

2 Transfer the bulgur wheat to a clean bowl and fluff it up with a fork. Add the tomatoes, cucumber, spring onions, olives, capers and herbs and toss gently. Stir in the olive oil and lemon juice, and season to taste with salt and pepper.

3 Crumble the feta over the top and serve.

VARIATIONS
- Stir in some bottled red or yellow (bell) peppers.
- Substitute chopped red onion for the spring onions (scallions).
- Stir in some toasted pine nuts and sprinkle with pomegranate seeds.

GREEK VEGAN SALAD BOWL

200g/7oz (1¼ cups) quinoa (dry weight)
480ml/16fl oz (2 cups) vegetable stock
½ red onion, diced
8 ripe baby plum tomatoes, halved
2 tbsp toasted pine nuts
2 tbsp pumpkin seeds
a handful of flat-leaf (Italian) parsley, chopped
1 ripe avocado, peeled, stoned (pitted) and diced
juice of 1 lemon
1–2 tbsp fruity olive oil
sea salt and freshly ground black pepper
1 quantity tomato fritters (see page 18)
vegan tzatziki, to serve (see page 24)

This healthy and hearty salad will fill you up whatever the weather. The quinoa is topped with crisp *domatokeftedes* (tomato fritters) and dairy-free vegan tzatziki. You can also add some shredded spinach or rocket leaves (arugula) if wished.

1 Rinse the quinoa in a sieve under cold running water, then drain. Heat the stock in a pan set over a high heat and when it starts to boil, tip in the quinoa. Reduce the heat to low, cover the pan and cook gently for 15 minutes, or until the quinoa is tender and has absorbed most of the liquid. It's cooked when the 'sprout' or 'tail' pops out of the seed.

2 Turn off the heat and leave the quinoa to steam in the pan for at least 5 minutes. Drain off any excess liquid and fluff it up with a fork.

3 Transfer the quinoa to a large bowl and stir in the onion, tomatoes, pine nuts, seeds, parsley, avocado, lemon juice and olive oil. Season to taste with salt and pepper.

4 Divide between 4 shallow serving bowls and top with the fried tomato fritters and tzatziki.

VARIATIONS
• Add some griddled vegan halloumi.
• Use bulgur wheat instead of quinoa.
• Substitute hummus for the tzatziki.

WARM POTATO SALAD

PATATA SALATA

SERVES 4–6
PREP: 15 MINUTES
COOK: 25–30 MINUTES

1kg/2¼lb potatoes, skins on
1 red onion, chopped or
    thinly sliced
1 bunch of flat-leaf (Italian)
    parsley, chopped
a handful of mint, chopped
50g/2oz juicy black olives
50g/2oz (¼ cup) capers,
    drained
sea salt and freshly ground
    black pepper

DRESSING:
120ml/4fl oz (½ cup) fruity
    extra virgin olive oil
juice of 1 lemon
1 tbsp red wine vinegar
1 garlic clove, crushed

This simple potato salad is so delicious and easy to make. It's the perfect accompaniment to grilled (broiled) fish and seafood or you can serve it as part of a buffet or meze spread. In Greece the best potatoes come from the Aegean island of Naxos, but you can use any firm waxy potatoes that hold their shape when boiled.

1 Put the potatoes in a large pan of salted water set over a high heat and bring to the boil. Cook for 25–30 minutes, or until tender. Drain well.

2 When the potatoes are cool enough to handle but still warm, peel them and cut into chunks.

3 Place in a bowl with the onion, herbs, olives and capers, and season with salt and pepper.

4 Put the dressing ingredients in a screw-top jar and screw on the lid. Shake well until combined and then pour over the warm potato salad.

5 Gently toss everything together. You want the potatoes to be still warm to soak up some of the dressing. Check the seasoning and serve warm, or leave to cool, then cover and keep in the fridge to serve later.

VARIATIONS
- Use chopped spring onions (scallions) instead of a red onion.
- Substitute dill for the mint.
- Add some dried or fresh oregano.
- Mix in some cooked prawns (shrimp) or chunks of canned tuna.

BAKING & DESSERTS

ΠΙΤΕΣ & ΓΛΥΚΑ

GREEK YOGHURT CAKE

SERVES 12
PREP: 15 MINUTES
COOK: 45–50
MINUTES

YAOURTOPITA

175g/6oz (¾ cup) unsalted butter, plus extra for greasing

225g/8oz (1 cup) caster (superfine) sugar

4 medium free-range eggs, separated

250g/9oz (1 cup) Greek yoghurt

225g/8oz (2 cups) plain (all-purpose) flour

3 tsp baking powder

¼ tsp bicarbonate of soda (baking soda)

a pinch of salt

grated zest and juice of 1 lemon

thick yoghurt, whipped cream or ice cream, to serve

SYRUP:

240ml/8fl oz (1 cup) water

225g/8oz (1 cup) caster (superfine) sugar

1 tsp rose water or orange blossom water

You're going to love this delicious cake, moistened with yoghurt and drenched in sweet, fragrant syrup. Better still, it's very quick and simple to make and you don't have to spend time decorating it. Serve it with tea or coffee as a snack, or with some fresh fruit as a dessert.

1 Preheat the oven to 180°C/350°F/gas mark 4. Butter a 23cm/9in square cake tin (baking pan) and line with baking parchment.

2 Beat the butter and sugar in a food mixer or with a hand-held electric whisk until fluffy and creamy. Beat in the egg yolks, one at a time, and then the yoghurt.

3 Sift in the flour, baking powder and bicarbonate of soda, and fold in gently with the salt, lemon zest and juice.

4 In a clean, dry bowl, whisk the egg whites until they are fluffy and form soft peaks. Gently fold into the cake mixture with a metal spoon, using a figure-of-eight motion, until all the egg white is incorporated.

5 Pour the mixture into the lined cake tin, level the top and bake in the preheated oven for 45–50 minutes, or until the cake is risen and golden brown on top. To test whether it's cooked, insert a thin skewer into the middle – if it comes out clean, it's ready. Leave in the tin to cool for a few minutes.

6 To make the syrup, put all the ingredients in a saucepan set over a medium heat and stir until the sugar dissolves. Increase the heat to high and boil for 4–5 minutes until thick and syrupy.

VARIATIONS
- Use orange zest and juice instead of lemon.
- Add a few drops of vanilla extract to the cake or the flower water.

7 Pour the hot syrup over the cake, a little at a time, so it sinks into the cake. When the cake is cold, cut it into diamond shapes or squares. Serve with thick yoghurt, whipped cream or ice cream.

Tip: We like to use Greek goat's yoghurt but cow's or sheep's yoghurt work well, too.

GREEK WALNUT CAKE

KARYTHOPITA

SERVES 12
PREP: 20 MINUTES
COOK: 40–50 MINUTES

butter, for greasing
475g/17oz (4¾ cups) shelled walnuts
3 slices of stale white bread
8 medium free-range eggs, separated
225g/8oz (1 cup) caster (superfine) sugar
4 tbsp brandy
grated zest of 1 orange
2 tsp baking powder
chopped walnuts, for sprinkling
vanilla ice cream or chilled yoghurt, to serve (optional)

This delicately spiced sticky cake is very healthy, being both fat- and gluten-free. Walnuts are an important crop in Greece and many homes have their own trees. The fresh, wet walnuts are harvested in the autumn (fall) and eaten with a glass of ouzo. Older dry walnuts are often ground and made into cakes to be enjoyed as a dessert or served with strong coffee or tea sweetened with honey.

1 Preheat the oven to 180°C/350°F/gas mark 4. Butter a 25cm/10in square cake tin (baking pan) or ovenproof Pyrex glass dish.

2 Blitz the walnuts in a food processor until finely ground but not powdered – the nuts should still retain some texture. Remove and set aside. Blitz the stale bread in the food processor or a blender until you have fine crumbs.

3 Using a food mixer or hand-held electric whisk, beat the egg yolks and sugar for 5 minutes, or until smooth, pale and fluffy. Then add the brandy and orange zest and beat for a further 30 seconds. Mix in the walnuts, breadcrumbs and baking powder.

4 Beat the egg whites in a clean, dry bowl until they are really thick and glossy and stand up in stiff peaks. Using a metal spoon, fold them gently, using a figure-of-eight movement, into the walnut mixture until everything is thoroughly combined.

SYRUP:
450g/1lb (2 cups) caster
   (superfine) sugar
420ml/14fl oz (1¾ cups)
   water
juice of 1 orange
1 cinnamon stick
4 whole cloves

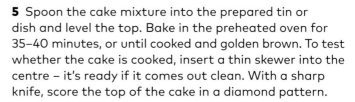

5 Spoon the cake mixture into the prepared tin or dish and level the top. Bake in the preheated oven for 35–40 minutes, or until cooked and golden brown. To test whether the cake is cooked, insert a thin skewer into the centre – it's ready if it comes out clean. With a sharp knife, score the top of the cake in a diamond pattern.

6 To make the syrup, put the sugar, water, orange juice, cinnamon stick and cloves in a saucepan and set over a medium heat. Stir with a wooden spoon until the sugar dissolves. Increase the heat and bring to the boil. As soon as it boils, reduce the heat to medium and cook for 5–10 minutes, or until it reduces and becomes syrupy. Discard the cinnamon stick and cloves.

7 Pour the hot syrup over the warm cake and sprinkle with chopped walnuts. Leave in the tin for about 1 hour until the cake is cold and all the syrup has been absorbed.

8 Cut into squares and serve with vanilla ice cream or chilled yoghurt, if you like. The cake will keep well for up to 5 days if stored in an airtight tin or container.

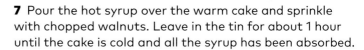

VARIATIONS
- Substitute lemon zest and juice for the orange.
- Add some ground cinnamon, ginger, allspice or cloves to the cake mixture.

APPLE FILO PIE

MILOPITA

SERVES 6
PREP: 15 MINUTES
COOK: 30–35
MINUTES

50g/2oz (¼ cup) unsalted butter, melted, plus extra for greasing
800g/1¾lb firm dessert apples, e.g. Granny Smith, peeled, cored and cubed
50g/2oz (generous ¼ cup) currants or sultanas (golden raisins)
grated zest of 1 lemon and a squeeze of juice
50g/2oz (¼ cup) soft light brown sugar
40g/1½oz (¼ cup) ground almonds (almond meal)
1 tsp ground cinnamon
a good pinch of freshly grated nutmeg
8 sheets ready-rolled filo (phyllo) pastry
25g/1oz (generous ¼ cup) flaked (slivered) almonds
icing (confectioner's) sugar, for dusting
thick and creamy Greek yoghurt, to serve

VARIATIONS
- Add some chopped walnuts to the filling.
- Add some ground allspice or cloves.

All Greeks have a sweet tooth, and they love pies, especially when the filling is wrapped in crisp, feather-light filo pastry. In Athens, the bakeries and pastry shops are always busy and long lines form on holidays and feast days. Depending on what fruit is in season, you could substitute plums, peaches or pears for the apples in this recipe.

1 Preheat the oven to 190°C/375°F/gas mark 5. Lightly butter a baking tray.

2 Put the apples, dried fruit, lemon zest and juice, sugar, ground almonds and spices in a bowl and mix well.

3 Spread a sheet of filo pastry out on a clean work surface and brush lightly with melted butter. Place another sheet on top and brush with more butter. Continue layering up the sheets in this way until they are all used. Cover the unused sheets with a damp tea (dish) towel while you work, to prevent them drying out.

4 Spoon the apple filling lengthways, along the centre of the filo pastry, in a long strip, not quite reaching the edge of the pastry at each end. Fold the ends of the pastry over the filling, and then fold one of the long sides over the filling, tucking it in neatly underneath. Brush with melted butter and then cover with the remaining pastry to make a sealed long parcel.

5 Lift the filo parcel, seam-side down, on to the buttered baking tray. Brush with the remaining melted butter and sprinkle with flaked almonds. Bake in the preheated oven for 30–35 minutes, or until the pastry is crisp and golden brown.

6 Dust with icing sugar and leave to cool a little. Serve the pie warm, cut into slices, with a dollop of creamy Greek yoghurt.

CHRISTMAS ALMOND COOKIES

MAKES APPROX. 80
PREP: 45 MINUTES
COOK: 25 MINUTES

KOURABIEDES

325g/11½oz (2 cups) whole
   almonds
480g/1lb 1oz (generous
   2 cups) cold unsalted
   butter, diced
150g/5oz (generous ½ cup)
   caster (superfine) sugar
1 large free-range egg yolk
85ml/3fl oz (scant ¾ cup)
   brandy
600g/1lb 5oz (scant 6 cups)
   self-raising (self-rising)
   flour, sifted
1.8kg/4lb (14 cups) icing
   (confectioner's) sugar
orange flower water, for
   brushing

These crisp, crumbly 'snowball' cookies are a Christmas delicacy. Every family has its own special recipe which has been handed down over several generations. The grandmothers (*yiayias*) make huge batches that are so delicious they soon disappear. Try them and see for yourself.

1 Preheat the oven to 180°C/350°F/gas mark 4.

2 Put the almonds in a bowl and cover them with boiling water. Leave for 1 minute, then drain and rinse in cold water. With your fingers, squeeze each almond out of its skin and pat dry with kitchen paper (paper towels).

3 Spread the almonds out on a baking tray and dry roast in the preheated oven for 7–10 minutes, or until fragrant and golden brown. Remove and cool. When they are cold, blitz them in a blender or food processor until coarsely – rather than finely – ground. You want them to have some texture.

4 Lower the oven temperature to 150°C/300°F/gas mark 2. Line 2 large baking trays with baking parchment.

5 Using a food mixer or hand-held electric whisk, beat the butter and caster sugar until white and fluffy. Beat in the egg yolk, followed by the ground almonds and brandy. Mix in the flour, a little at a time, until you have a soft but firm dough.

6 Divide the dough into small pieces, about the size of a walnut, and mould each one into a little ball, then flatten it slightly. Place the balls on the lined baking trays – not too close together as they will spread out a little while they cook.

VARIATIONS
- Add a little *masticha* or vanilla extract.
- Brush with rose water instead of orange flower water.

7 Bake in the centre of the preheated oven for 25 minutes, or until they are dry on the outside. Check on them after 15 minutes and if they are colouring, turn the baking trays the other way round or lower the oven temperature. The *kourabiedes* will be soft when you take them out of the oven but will crisp up as they cool.

8 Dust a baking sheet with plenty of sifted icing sugar. While the *kourabiedes* are still hot, place them on the sheet and lightly brush with orange flower water, then generously dredge with more sifted icing sugar to coat them all over. They should be completely covered. Leave to cool.

9 Store them in a biscuit tin or airtight container and leave for at least a day before serving, dusting lightly with more icing sugar. The *kourabiedes* will stay fresh for up to 1 month.

GREEK YOGHURT CHOCOLATE MOUSSE

SERVES 4
PREP: 10 MINUTES
CHILL: 1–2 HOURS

300g/10oz (1¼ cups) unsweetened Greek yoghurt
300g/10oz (1½ cups) low-fat cream cheese
4 tbsp cocoa powder
2 tsp liquid stevia
3 tbsp agave syrup
100g/3½oz (⅔ cup) skinned unsalted hazelnuts
100g/3½oz (⅔ cup) skinned unsalted almonds
dark chocolate shavings and raspberries, to decorate

It takes only a few minutes to whip up this creamy yet crunchy mousse. You can make it in advance and just leave it to chill and set in the fridge until you're ready to eat. Unlike a classic mousse it does not contain eggs or sugar.

1 Put the yoghurt, cream cheese, cocoa, stevia and agave syrup in a food processor or blender. Blend on a low speed for 3 minutes.

2 Transfer to a serving bowl and stir in the whole nuts. Cover and chill in the fridge for 1–2 hours until set firm.

3 Just before serving, decorate the mousse with chocolate shavings and raspberries.

Tip: Leaving the nuts whole gives the mousse a nice crunch.

VARIATIONS
• Use walnuts instead of hazelnuts or almonds.
• Add some grated orange zest or Grand Marnier.
• Serve with chocolate chip *cantuccini* (almond biscotti) or almond tuiles biscuits.

NO-BAKE CHOCOLATE 'SALAMI'

SERVES 6–8
PREP: 15 MINUTES
CHILL: 2+ HOURS

MOSAIKO

200g/7oz digestive biscuits
(Graham crackers)
250g/9oz (generous 1 cup)
unsalted butter, at room
temperature
4 tbsp cocoa powder, plus
extra for dusting
400ml/14fl oz (scant
1¾ cups) condensed milk
4 tsp brandy
100g/3½oz walnut halves,
coarsely chopped

Also known as *kormos* (tree trunk) in Greek, this no-cook chocolate log is one of the easiest desserts you can make. When it's sliced and the crushed biscuit pieces are revealed it resembles a mosaic – hence the name.

1 Take a 23 x 10cm/9 x 4in shallow baking tin (pan) and lay a large sheet of clingfilm (plastic wrap) on top.

2 Crush the biscuits in a bowl. Use your hands or bash them with a rolling pin. They should stay in small pieces, not powdery crumbs. Stir in the walnuts.

3 Using a wooden spoon, combine the softened butter and cocoa powder until well mixed. Add the condensed milk and brandy, and then transfer to a blender and blitz until smooth.

4 Stir the mixture into the crushed biscuits and walnuts, mixing well to distribute everything evenly.

5 Spoon the mixture on to the lined baking tin and shape it with your hands into a long sausage-shaped cylinder. Place it on long side of the tin and fold the clingfilm over the top, then roll it up in the clingfilm and twist the ends together to seal it.

6 Chill in the fridge for at least 2 hours until firm and set. Dust with cocoa powder and serve cut into slices with a cup of strong coffee, or as a dessert with ice cream.

VARIATIONS
- Stir some melted dark chocolate into the mixture before rolling into a cylinder.
- Add some grated orange zest and use orange liqueur instead of brandy.
- Add a few drops of vanilla extract.

CHRISTMAS HONEY COOKIES

MAKES APPROX.
40 COOKIES
PREP: 30 MINUTES
COOL: 3 HOURS
COOK: 20 MINUTES

MELOMAKARONA

150g/5oz (¾ cup) fine semolina (dry weight)

500g/1lb 2oz (5 cups) plain (all-purpose) flour, sifted

2 tsp baking powder

100g/3½oz (½ cup) caster (superfine) sugar

180ml (¾ cup) fresh orange juice

4 tbsp brandy, e.g. Metaxa

2 tsp ground cinnamon

½ tsp ground nutmeg

½ tsp ground cloves

1 tsp bicarbonate of soda (baking soda)

240ml/8fl oz (1 cup) olive oil

2 tbsp water

3 tbsp clear honey

grated zest of 2 oranges

finely chopped or ground walnuts, for sprinkling

ground cinnamon, for dusting

These fragrant, spicy cookies are always eaten at Christmas in Greece. You need to make the honey syrup at least 3 hours in advance, if not the day before, so that it is completely cold by the time you take the _melomakarona_ out of the oven. The piping-hot cookies will quickly absorb the cold syrup and become deliciously moist.

1 To make the syrup, put the water, sugar, spices and orange halves in a pan and set over a medium heat (see page 124 for continued ingredients list). Stir until the sugar melts and then bring to the boil. Boil for 4–5 minutes, then remove from the heat and stir in the honey. Set aside for at least 3 hours or until the syrup is cold.

2 Preheat the oven to 180°C/350°F/gas mark 4. Line 4 baking trays with baking parchment.

3 Put the semolina, flour and baking powder in a bowl and mix well together.

4 In another bowl, beat the sugar, orange juice, brandy, ground spices and bicarbonate of soda with a hand whisk until well mixed. Whisk in the oil, water, honey and orange zest.

5 Tip in the flour mixture and, using your hands, mix gently until everything comes together to form a soft dough. Knead quickly and lightly until smooth. Do not over-mix or over-knead.

Continued overleaf →

SYRUP:

300ml/½ pint (1¼ cups)
   water
600g/1lb 5oz (2½ cups)
   granulated sugar
2 cinnamon sticks
3 cloves
1 orange, cut in half
200g/7oz (generous
   ½ cup) honey

6 Take small amounts (about 30g/1oz) of the dough and shape each one into an oval cookie. Place on the lined baking trays and bake in the preheated oven for 20 minutes, or until golden brown.

7 Immediately, using a slotted spoon, dip the hot cookies into the cold syrup and soak for 10–20 seconds before transferring to a wire rack to cool. Sprinkle with chopped or ground walnuts and dust lightly with ground cinnamon.

8 Store the cookies in an airtight tin or container. They will keep well for up to 3 weeks in a cool place.

> **Tip: Knead the dough lightly until it is soft – don't overwork it or the cookies will be very oily.**

INDEX

Note: page numbers in **bold** refer to illustrations.

Published in 2023 by Ebury Press an imprint of Ebury Publishing,
20 Vauxhall Bridge Road,
London SW1V 2SA

Ebury Press is part of the Penguin Random House group of companies
whose addresses can be found at global.penguinrandomhouse.com

Text © Ebury Press 2023
Design © Ebury Press 2023
Photography © Ebury Press 2023

Photography: Haarala Hamilton
Food Stylist: Jake Fenton
Assistant Food Stylist: Hattie Baker
Prop Stylist: Daisy Shayler-Webb
Design: Louise Evans
Production: Rebecca Jones and Emily Casey
Publishing Director: Elizabeth Bond

This edition first published by Ebury Press in 2023

www.penguin.co.uk

A CIP catalogue record for this book is available from the British Library

ISBN 978-1-52914-919-7

Printed and bound in China by Toppan Leefung